PEOPLES
of
EASTERN ASIA

Mongolia

Myanmar

Nepal

PEOPLES
of
EASTERN ASIA

Volume 8
Mongolia–Nepal

MARSHALL CAVENDISH
NEW YORK • LONDON • SINGAPORE

Marshall Cavendish Corporation
99 White Plains Road
Tarrytown, New York 10591
www.marshallcavendish.com

Consultants:
Emily K. Bloch, Department of South Asian Languages and Civilizations, University of Chicago
Amy Rossabi, MA in Southeast Asian History
Morris Rossabi, Professor and Senior Research Scholar, Columbia University

Contributing authors:
Fiona Macdonald
Gillian Stacey
Philip Steele

Marshall Cavendish
Editor: Marian Armstrong
Editorial Director: Paul Bernabeo
Production Manager: Michael Esposito

Discovery Books
Managing Editor: Paul Humphrey
Project Editor: Kate Taylor
Design Concept: Ian Winton
Designer: Barry Dwyer
Cartographer: Stefan Chabluk
Picture Researcher: Laura Durman

The publishers would like to thank the following for their permission to reproduce photographs:
akg-images: 412, 428, 429, 454 (Puppentheat.Mus.Berlin: 444); CORBIS (Richard Bailey: 410; Dean Conger: 419, 422; Corbis SYGMA: 430; Ric Ergenbright: 451; Macduff Everton: 457; Craig Lovell: 459 bottom; Richard Powers: 431; Keren Su: cover; Nevada Wier: 424; Alison Wright: 460); Eye Ubiquitous (David Cumming: 435, 437 bottom; John Dakers: 427; Bennett Dean: 462); Hutchison Library (Stephen Pern: 414, 418); James Davis Photography: 453; James Davis Travel Photography: 459 top, 463; Panos (Jean-Léo Dugast: 442 top; Jeremy Horner: 436); Still Pictures (Toby Adamson: 417; Adrian Arbib: 416; COLPHOTO: 442 bottom; Venetia Dearden: 434 bottom; Jean-Léo Dugast: 439; Ton Koene: 415; Liverani-UNEP: 434 top; Stephen Pern: 421 bottom, 423 top; Peter Schickert: 437 top; Hartmut Schwarzbach: 448; Jorgen Schytte: 455, 456, 458); Trip (M. Barlow: 423 bottom; T. Bognar: 440, 441, 447; Graham Grieves: 432, 443, 445; W. Jacobs: 461; David Pluth: 421 top)

(cover) A woman practices martial arts in Beijing, China.

Editor's note: Many systems of dating have been used by different cultures throughout history. *Peoples of Eastern Asia* uses B.C.E. (Before Common Era) and C.E. (Common Era) instead of B.C. (Before Christ) and A.D. (Anno Domini, "In the Year of the Lord").

Library of Congress Cataloging-in-Publication Data

Peoples of Eastern Asia.
    p. cm.
    Includes bibliographical references and index.
    Contents: v. 1. Bangladesh-Brunei -- v. 2. Cambodia-China -- v. 3. China-East Timor -- v. 4. India -- v. 5. Indonesia -- v. 6. Japan-Korea, North -- v. 7. Korea, South-Malaysia -- v. 8. Mongolia-Nepal -- v. 9. Philippines-Sri Lanka -- v. 10. Taiwan-Vietnam.
    ISBN 0-7614-7547-8 (set : alk. paper) -- ISBN 0-7614-7548-6 (v. 1 : alk. paper) -- ISBN 0-7614-7549-4 (v. 2 : alk. paper) -- ISBN 0-7614-7550-8 (v. 3 : alk. paper) -- ISBN 0-7614-7551-6 (v. 4 : alk. paper) -- ISBN 0-7614-7552-4 (v. 5 : alk. paper) -- ISBN 0-7614-7553-2 (v. 6 : alk. paper) -- ISBN 0-7614-7554-0 (v. 7 : alk. paper) -- ISBN 0-7614-7555-9 (v. 8 : alk. paper) -- ISBN 0-7614-7556-7 (v. 9 : alk. paper) -- ISBN 0-7614-7557-5 (v. 10 : alk. paper) -- ISBN 0-7614-7558-3 (v. 11 : index vol. : alk. paper)
    1. East Asia. 2. Asia, Southeastern. 3. South Asia. 4. Ethnology--East Asia. 5. Ethnology--Asia, Southeastern. 6. Ethnology--South Asia.

DS511.P457 2004
950--dc22

2003069645

    ISBN 0-7614-7547-8 (set : alk. paper)
    ISBN 0-7614-7555-9 (v. 8 : alk. paper)

Printed in China
09 08 07 06 05 04   6 5 4 3 2 1

Contents

MONGOLIA

MONGOLIA IS A LANDLOCKED COUNTRY IN EAST-CENTRAL ASIA.

The landscape consists of high, rolling steppes (grass-covered plains), crossed by mountain ridges. There are many salt and freshwater lakes, and also mineral springs. Rough grass covers the plains, and there are forests on the mountain slopes. The Gobi Desert occupies about a third of the country.

Most of Mongolia is wild, uncultivated countryside, but there are increasing environmental problems.

KAZAKHSTAN
RUSSIA
CHINA
Hövsgöl Nuur
Darhan
Choybalsan
Ulaangom
Erdenet
★ULAANBAATAR
Hovd
MONGOLIA
GOBI DESERT
Dalandzadgad
CHINA

N

miles 0 — 200
km 0 — 300

CLIMATE

Mongolia has a harsh climate. On average, there are 260 sunny days each year. Winters are extremely cold, with temperatures down to –26°F (–32°C). There are high winds and dust storms in spring, followed by summer rains. Summers are cool, except in the desert, where daytime temperatures can reach 110°F (43°C).

	Ulaanbaatar
Average January temperature:	–12°F (–24°C)
Average July temperature:	62°F (17°C)
Average annual precipitation:	10 in. (25 cm)

A typical Mongolian landscape, with cattle grazing on steppes and high mountains with sparse forests.

Early Mongolia

The first traces of human settlement in Mongolia (mawn-GOE-lee-uh) have been found in the Gobi (GOE-bee) Desert. They date from around 500,000–200,000 B.C.E. Archaeological evidence shows that around 3000–1500 B.C.E. peoples in Mongolia tamed horses, yaks, and camels, and by 1000 B.C.E. they had learned to make bronze. By around 300 B.C.E. they had strong, sharp iron weapons, which they used to attack their neighbors, especially China. With other warlike tribes, mostly of Mongol ethnic origin, they roamed across a vast area of north-central Asia. Their homeland stretched from what is now Korea to Kazakhstan (KAH-zahk-stahn) and had few fixed borders.

Mongol peoples continued to make raids on China, and also fought among themselves. Then in 907 C.E. one ambitious Mongol tribe, the Khitans (KEE-tahnz), invaded part of northern China, where they remained until 1115. They also seized control of the region of present-day Mongolia. In 1206 a Mongol chieftain named Temujin declared himself *Genghis Khan* (Universal Ruler). He forced all Mongol tribes to accept him as their leader and set out to win new lands. By the time he died, in 1227, Mongol armies had conquered an empire stretching from the western borders of China to the Caspian Sea.

In 1240 Genghis Kahn's son, Ögödei, sent Mongol armies to Russia and Hungary. Ögödei's nephew, Hulegu, made further conquests in the Middle East, capturing the splendid Muslim city of Baghdad in 1258. The Mongols' advance west and south was finally halted by Muslim troops from Egypt in 1260, but this did not stop further Mongol conquests in the east. In 1279 Mongol leader Kublai Khan conquered China and founded a dynasty of emperors there known as the Yuan (yuh-WAHN).

The Mongol empire now stretched from Korea to Hungary, and was the largest the world had ever seen. Such a vast area was impossible to defend. In 1368 a new dynasty of emperors, the Ming, won control in China and drove the Mongols back

---

FACTS AND FIGURES

Official name: *Republic of Mongolia*

Status: *Independent state*

Capital: *Ulaanbaatar*

Major towns: *Darhan, Erdenet, Choybalsan*

Area: *604,247 square miles (1,564,994 square kilometers)*

Population: *2,450,000*

Population density: *4 per square mile (2 per square kilometer)*

Peoples: *85 percent Mongol (mostly Khalkha); 7 percent Turkic (mostly Kazakhs); 8 percent others, including Chinese and Russian*

Official language: *Khalkha Mongol*

Currency: *Tugrik*

National day: *Independence Day/Revolution Day (July 11)*

Country's name: *Mongolia is named after the Mongol people. It is also known as "Land of Blue Sky."*

Time line:	First inhabitants of Gobi Desert region	First iron weapons in Mongolia	Khitan Mongols attack China
	500,000–200,000 B.C.E.	300 B.C.E.	907

Kublai Khan (1215–1294) led Mongolian armies to conquer southern China. He also invaded Korea and Myanmar and led ambitious but unsuccessful attacks on Java and Japan.

toward the region of present-day Mongolia. Once there, rival Mongol groups began once again to fight among themselves. Other groups of Mongols remained in China, under Chinese rule.

A new strong leader, Altan Khan, fought (and lost) a war against China. He also attacked Tibet. During his campaigns he became fascinated by Buddhism, and instead of destroying Tibet, he invited Buddhist monks to Mongolia. Altan also tried to reunite the Mongols. However, after his death, Mongol groups fought among each other once again.

Chinese Rule

Meanwhile, in China, a powerful new dynasty, the Qing (CHING), from Manchuria, seized power. When the Khalkha (KAHL-kah) Mongol tribes asked

for their help to fight Mongol rivals, the armies of the Qing invaded Mongolia, using muskets (early handheld rifles) and cannons. Mongol soldiers could not defend themselves, and by 1691 all of Mongolia was under Chinese control.

The Qing conquerors divided the land where the Mongols lived into two separate regions—Inner Mongolia (part of China) and Outer Mongolia (approximately the same area as the nation of Mongolia today). They ruled both harshly, levying heavy taxes and imposing cruel punishments. As a result, many Mongolian people still feel hostile toward China today.

By 1911 the Qing government faced a crisis in China. A group of Mongolian nobles seized the opportunity to declare Outer Mongolia's independence on December 1. They appointed the eighth *Jebtzun Damba* (Mongolian Buddhist leader) as ruler of the new nation, which they named Mongolia, and gave him a new title, *Bogd Khan* (Holy King). The Mongolians appealed to their neighbors, Russia and China, to respect their right to rule themselves, but both had ambitions to seize Mongolia for themselves.

After the Communist Revolution in Russia (1917), Mongolia became a battleground as Chinese, then Russians, invaded. In 1921 Mongolians, backed by Bolsheviks (BOEL-sheh-vihkz: Russian communist revolutionaries), declared Mongolia to be an Independent People's Government. Mongolia's first political

Genghis Khan unites Mongol tribes	Kublai Khan conquers China and founds Yuan dynasty	War between Mongol tribes in Mongolia	Rule of Altan Khan; he invades Tibet and brings back Buddhism to Mongolia
1206	1279	1400–1454	1543–1583

party, the Mongolian People's Party, set up a new government. The Bogd Khan stayed on as head of state, but he had little power.

Communist Mongolia

In 1924 Mongolian communist politicians set up a new Mongolian People's Republic, making Mongolia the world's second communist state. Officially Mongolia was independent of the Soviet Union, but when Soviet dictator Joseph Stalin came to power in 1924, he exterminated all Mongolian politicians who did not support his views. Those who remained, led by Mongolian Khorloogiyn Choibalsan, head of the *Little Khural* (KHOOR-ahl: Government Assembly), followed Stalinist policies, killing Buddhist monks and critics of the government. More than 27,000 citizens had been killed by 1939.

The Stalinist government also introduced collectivization plans. Under these, land was shared among Mongolian people, who were forced to give up their way of life and join cooperative farming or industrial projects. Private businesses were banned, and foreign traders (mostly Chinese) were expelled. These upheavals led to terrible famine, and thousands more Mongolians died.

In 1931, as part of its plans for a new Far Eastern empire, Japan prepared to invade Mongolia. Stalin sent Soviet troops there and forced large numbers of nomads to join the Mongolian army. The Japanese invaded Mongolia in 1939, but they were beaten back. However, the Soviet army stayed in Mongolia, and Stalin used its presence to force the Chinese government to finally accept Mongolia's independence in 1946.

In 1952 Mongolian leader Choibalsan died, and a new, less harsh communist government ruled in his place, but links between Mongolia and the U.S.S.R. remained strong. Mongolian students studied at Russian universities. Russian-style food, music, and theater all came to Mongolia for the first time.

Reforming Soviet leader Mikhail Gorbachev recalled Soviet troops from Mongolia in 1986. Mongolian communist leaders began to copy his policies of glasnost (openness) and perestroika (economic and social reorganization). In March 1990 crowds of Mongolians gathered in the capital, Ulaanbaatar (oo-LAHN bah-TAHR), to demand democracy. The communist government resigned.

Mongolia Today

Multiparty elections were held in July 1990. City dwellers supported new, democratic parties, but the majority of Mongolians, living in the countryside, voted the former communist leaders back into power. The leaders passed new laws, allowing freedom of speech and religious toleration, but without Soviet aid, the Mongolian economy soon faced collapse. The new government called fresh elections in 1992 and again won power.

The economic crisis worsened, and in 1996 an alliance of noncommunist parties, the Mongolian Democratic Coalition, was elected. They introduced economic reforms, encouraging free trade and private

All of Mongolia under Chinese control	Mongolians declare independence from China	Mongolians and Russian Bolsheviks defeat Chinese	Mongolia becomes world's second Communist People's Republic; strict communist rule
1691	**1911**	**1921**	**1924**

This man from the Buryat Mongol minority is dressed for the freezing Mongolian winter in a coat of fleecy sheepskin, a sheepskin cap, and sheepskin boots.

enterprise. These reforms made some businesspeople very rich, but they drove ordinary Mongolians further into poverty. There were accusations of corruption among business leaders and politicians. Democratic leaders also often quarreled among themselves—there were five prime ministers between 1996 and 2000. When further elections were called in 2000, the former communist Mongolian People's Revolutionary Party was once more voted into power.

Mongolia is now peaceful and free from repressive government or foreign control, but it is desperately poor. Many Mongolians seem prepared to live simply, like their ancestors. Others, however, are eager to modernize their nation and share in the wealth and opportunities of the modern world, even if this risks destroying their unique way of life.

Peoples of Mongolia

Most people living in Mongolia are ethnic Mongols belonging to the Khalkha group. There are also around 47,000 members of the *Buryat* (BUHR-ee-aht) group of Mongols living in the north and west and around 32,000 belonging to the Dariganga Mongols living in the far southeast.

There are also ethnic minorities in Mongolia. The largest group is the Kazakhs (kah-ZAHKS), numbering around 130,000. Living mostly in the west of the country, they share a similar lifestyle to the Mongols.

Many are nomads who keep sheep and goats; others live as hunters, riding on horseback and using eagles to catch small animals for food.

Nomadic Life

The peoples of Mongolia have a long history as nomads. They once had no settled homes, living instead in large dome-shaped tents, called *gers* (GUHRZ). Nomad families moved from place to place several times a year to find fresh grazing land for their horses, camels, yaks, sheep, and goats.

Japan invades Mongolia	Mongolian communist ruler Choibalsan dies; new, less strict policies by rulers	Calls for democracy end communist rule	Time of political instability and economic decline
1939	**1952**	**1990**	**1992–2000**

During the communist era, all Mongolians were encouraged to give up this nomadic way of life and settle in cities and towns, but this policy did not succeed.

Today around half of all Mongolians live in the traditional way. Many more families, settled in towns, leave their homes in concrete apartment buildings during the summertime to camp in the open countryside. Others live in gers year-round, but on settled campgrounds on the outskirts of cities and towns.

Each ger is made of thick felt cloth arranged over a collapsible wooden frame. With several people helping—moving camp was traditionally women's work—a ger can be put up or taken down in two or three hours. In summer the walls can be rolled up to allow cool breezes to blow inside. In winter extra layers of felt are added for insulation. If a family is poor, bare earth is the only flooring, but wealthier families have wooden floors. The doorway, also made of wood and often painted, always faces south.

The inside of each ger is arranged in much the same way. A metal stove stands in the center, and a small table and stools are arranged close by. Low beds, wooden storage chests, and all kinds of useful items line the walls, and a portable Buddhist altar

A village of snow-covered gers (felt tents) is buffeted by the strong winds that sweep across the Mongolian steppes in winter.

Kazakh Eagle-Hunters

For thousands of years Kazakh people have captured wild eagles and used them to hunt foxes, marmots (small rodents), and young wolves. Hunters catch young female birds, let them become used to human company, and then train them. The eagles have a natural instinct to catch prey, but they have to be taught to share it with their owners by a system of rewards. Most hunters keep their trained birds for about ten years before releasing them into the wild, where they may live for another twenty years or more.

also hangs there. Behind the stove, facing the door, is the place of honor, where old people and visitors sit. For everyone else, space inside the ger is sharply divided. Men occupy the left-hand side or western half; women sit and work in the right-hand side or eastern half.

Nomadic life is hard for men, women, and children. Their camps have no gas, electricity, or water supplies, and no bathrooms, although settled campsites may have a communal bathhouse, called a *khaluun us* (kah-LOON-uhs). Fires are essential and are used for cooking and keeping warm, but wood is scarce on the steppe grasslands. Women and girls

Livestock are Mongolian farmers' most prized possessions. This Mongol is helping to vaccinate a herd of horses against disease.

theaters, bars, nightclubs, museums, and a few ancient monasteries.

There are also markets, stores, government buildings, offices, and factories, where many people work, although unemployment is a serious problem, affecting two out of every five city adults. Citizens live in suburbs of concrete apartment buildings or in outer districts of ger camps. Homeless and destitute people, including thousands of street children, seek refuge in underground sewers and heating pipes or in shelters run by aid agencies.

collect dried dung to use for fuel. They also fetch water from lakes and streams for cooking and washing.

Families depend on their animals, and caring for them takes up a large part of every day. Men look after the horses; boys herd flocks of sheep and goats. Women do the milking and make yogurt, cheese, and butter. They also comb soft hair from cashmere goats for clothes and make felt from sheep's wool.

City Life

About one-third of the Mongolian population — more than 750,000 people — lives in or around the capital city, Ulaanbaatar. City life is very different from life in the countryside. There are paved streets, electricity, piped water, and drains. City districts are bustling with Western-style hotels, playhouses, movie

Traditional Clothes

As a sign of national identity, many Mongolians still like to wear traditional clothing. Men and women wear a del *(DEHL), a long woolen coat with a wrap-over front and a high collar, tied around the waist with a sash. There are several different regional styles. With the del, Mongolians wear tall* gutul *(goo-TOOL: boots) of embroidered leather, with curved toes — or sometimes heavy modern boots, which are more practical. Men wear hats of fox fur or wolf skin, or Russian-style caps, and women wear thick, brightly colored scarves.*

Kazakh people dress differently. Men wear baggy shirts and pants, vests, and long cloaks. Women wear long dresses, with embroidered velvet vests and heavy jewelry of silver and semiprecious stones. On their heads most Kazakh people wear embroidered skullcaps, though older women sometimes wear headscarves. In winter men also wear hats made of fur.

There are around five thousand homeless children in Mongolia. They have been abandoned by their parents, who cannot afford to care for them.

Mongolians live, such as China. Mongolian used to be written in a rounded, flowing script, from the top to the bottom of the page, but in 1944 Mongolian script was replaced by the Russian Cyrillic (suh-RIHL-ihk) alphabet. This is still used today.

The minority peoples in Mongolia speak their own languages. Most, such as Kazakh, are from the Turkic language group. Because Mongolia was influenced by the U.S.S.R. for much of the twentieth century, some older Mongolians speak Russian. Today many young Mongolian people are keen to learn English.

In several districts of Mongolia there are large industrial complexes where mineral ores are mined. The biggest is at Erdenet (UHR-duh-neht), in northern Mongolia, where a whole mountain of copper-bearing rock is being quarried. About eight thousand workers and their families live there. At Erdes (UHR-dehz), in eastern Mongolia, there is a ghost town, built in communist times, where thousands of Russians and Mongolians once worked in a uranium mine. It closed in 1998, after the Russian government ran out of money to operate it.

Language

Mongolian, or Khalkha Mongol, is related to other languages spoken in Asia, such as Turkish and Korean. Nine out of ten people in Mongolia speak it. There are several different dialects in regions of Mongolia and also in other countries where

Let's Talk Mongolian

Sain baina uu (SAEN BIE-nuh OO)	*Hello*
Tany neriig ken geded ve? (TAH-nee nuh-RIHG kuhn GEH-dehd veh)	*What is your name?*
Tanai ger buliinhen sain u? (tuh-NIE guh bool-YEEN-uhn SAIN OO)	*How is your family?*
Ta ali ulssaas irsen be? (TAH-lee ool-SAHS EER-suhm BEH)	*What country are you from?*
Ta nadad tsuslana uu? (TAH nuh-DAHD zoo-LAH-nuh OO)	*Could you help me please?*
Bayarlalaa (BIE-yahr-luh-LAH)	*Thank you*
Bayartai (BIE-yahr-TIE)	*Goodbye*

Religion

Since prehistoric times, Mongolian people have been animists. They worship nature spirits, in animals, mountains, rivers, and trees. They especially honor the sky spirit, Tengrii (TEHNG-gree), and build *ovoo* (OE-voo: pyramid-shaped piles of stones, topped with offerings) to please him. Shamans (magic healers) act as links between people and the spirit world, and many believe they can cure illness caused by spirits. Living alone, and always rather feared, they dance, fall into trances, and sacrifice animals as part of their cures.

Over the past five hundred years, these ancient animist beliefs have been combined with the Tibetan branch of the Buddhist faith. Mongol leader Altan Khan made Buddhism the Mongolian state religion. Powerful Chinese and Mongol families gave money to build hundreds of temple monasteries and sent their sons there. By the beginning of the twentieth century, more than 100,000 men — one in three of the Mongolian male population — were Buddhist monks.

In temple monasteries monks learned secret religious teachings that were said to be too precious for ordinary people to understand. They also provided education. Over the years temple monasteries became extremely powerful, controlling large areas of land and owning many rich treasures. Ordinary people were forced to work for them.

Monks honored lamas (religious teachers and leaders), whom they believed had been reborn from previous lives. They called them Living Buddhas. The most important was the Jebtzun Damba, head of all Mongolian Buddhists and the third most important Buddhist teacher in the world.

After around 1600 the Buddhist faith spread to ordinary Mongolians, although many people understood it in only a limited way. They said prayers to "compassionate Buddhas," holy people from the past who delayed their entry to nirvana — the Buddhist state of selfless bliss — to help others. Their favorite was Tara, the merciful.

When the communists came to power in Mongolia in 1921 they tried to abolish all religions. They especially disliked the

An ovoo (stone pyramid) in the mountains of western Mongolia. Worshipers walk three times around an ovoo, place an offering on top, and make a wish.

A Buddhist monk lies on a prayer board at the Gandan Monastery in Ulaanbaatar. He is holding a string of 108 beads; each one represents a different prayer.

monasteries because of their links with past rulers. Monks did not work, marry, or have children, so the communists blamed them for Mongolia's poverty and falling population. The communists destroyed many monasteries and killed many monks.

Since the fall of the U.S.S.R. (early 1990s), religions have again become popular. Mongolian families have Buddhist altars, where they say prayers and make offerings. They walk three times around the ovoo, leave gifts for spirits, and then make a wish.

There are also small communities of Christians—encouraged by foreign missionaries—and around 100,000 Muslims, mostly among the Kazakh minority.

Tsagaan Sar (White Month Festival)

Tsagaan Sar celebrates the Mongolian New Year, which is calculated by the lunar calendar. It takes place in January or February and lasts for three days. On the first day a fat sheep is killed. Its meat is used to make hundreds of special stuffed dumplings, which are offered to visitors and eaten at family feasts. On the last day people eat the tail — the fattest part. People spend the festival eating, drinking, singing traditional songs, visiting monasteries, and offering traditional greetings, called zolgogh *(ZOHL-gock), to older people.*

Society and Economy

Mongolian people have welcomed many features of modern life, especially education and communications systems. Many nomad families have battery-powered radios to keep in touch with national events from remote campsites. Like other nomadic peoples, they prize their freedom and independence, and they still admire ancient warrior qualities such as bravery, loyalty, and endurance. They respect traditional customs, including hospitality to guests, help to friends and strangers in need, and reverence of the elderly. They celebrate many traditional festivals, the most important being *Naadam* (nah-DAHM), in July, which features traditional sports, parades, music, and dancing. Mongolians traditionally allow women greater freedom than many other Asian societies. Women can get an education, have a career, head households, manage animals, and appear freely in public.

For many centuries Mongolian people measured their wealth by the number of animals they owned and the condition of their grazing lands. Even today, almost half the population of Mongolia depends on livestock rearing. There are around fifteen million sheep, eleven million goats, and over three million horses in Mongolia. Families with large herds can live reasonably comfortably, providing their own food, breeding animals, and selling wool, hair, meat, and skins, but families with small herds often struggle to survive. All farmers are vulnerable to *zud* (ZOOD: extreme bad weather). The last zud happened in 2002, when around ten million animals died.

Mongolia has rich mineral resources of copper, coal, molybdenum (a metallic element used to strengthen steel), tin, tungsten, and gold, and several oil fields. Mining and metalworking are Mongolia's biggest industries, earning more than 70 percent of the nation's export income and employing one-third of the workforce.

Mongolia has few other industries, apart from cement making and processing animal by-products, such as leather. Tourism is increasingly important. However, without help from other nations, Mongolia would not survive. Until 1990 the U.S.S.R. gave Mongolia large amounts of aid, but this ended after the Soviet Union collapsed, causing Mongolia's economy to sink into a deep recession.

In 1996 leaders of the new democratic government introduced sweeping free-trade reforms and negotiated new packages of international aid from the International Monetary Fund, the World Bank, and the Asian Development Bank. Today Mongolia is the fifth largest recipient of aid in the world. However, large debts, plus political quarrels, have left most overseas businesses unwilling to invest in Mongolia. Falling international prices of Mongolia's chief exports, copper and cashmere goat hair, have caused further problems. The government elected in 2000 has promised new plans to encourage business, but it is still too soon to know whether these will be successful. Meanwhile, four out of every ten Mongolian citizens live in poverty.

Soup and Noodles

Traditional Mongolian food is plain and simple. In the winter, families eat boiled mutton (sheep) with *buuz* (BOOZ: flour dumplings), mutton soup with noodles, or *khuushuur* (koo-SHOOR: fried pancakes stuffed with chopped mutton). In the summer, dairy products such as tangy yogurt, chewy dried milk curds, sharp-

---

Soyombo

This design has symbolized the Mongolian state since Genghis Khan's time. It appears on official documents and the national flag.
From top to bottom, its design means:

- *three flames = past, present, future*
- *disc = sun*
- *crescent = moon*
- *triangle = arrowhead (victory)*
- *rectangle = integrity*
- *interlocking shapes in circle = earth, sky, fire, water*
- *rectangle = honesty*
- *triangle = arrowhead (victory)*
- *two vertical bars = friendship*

This Mongolian woman crouches on the floor of her home, in a ger, to cook tasty fried pancakes, a favorite Mongolian snack.

potatoes, onions, and cabbages, in fields close to cities and towns.

The most popular beverage in Mongolia is tea. It is served black or with milk and sugar and almost always with added salt. In the countryside many nomadic families still make traditional beverages from fermented milk. *Airag* (ie-RAHG) is sour, fizzy, and mildly alcoholic; *shimiin arkhi* (shih-MEEN ahr-KEE) is a very powerful liquor. Instant coffee, mineral water, and fruit juices are available in towns, where there are also many breweries making beer and distilleries producing vodka.

Also in towns there are markets and stores selling Russian-style foods, including bread, biscuits, sugar, tomato sauce, and vegetables pickled in vinegar. In the biggest cities restaurants and fast-food stores sell Western-style burgers and also Korean, Indian, and Chinese meals. Throughout the country there are Mongolian *guanz* (GWANZ: canteens), selling tea, soup, and mutton.

flavored soft cheese, and thick cream are the most usual foods. They are made with milk from sheep, goats, cows, or camels and served with bread.

For special occasions, whole goats or marmots are cooked by being filled with red-hot stones and then roasted over a fire. *Khorkhog* (koer-KAWG), a special mutton stew, is made by dropping hot stones into a pot of mutton and water. Strips of dried meat, called *borts* (BOERTZ), or sausages made of horse and camel meat are also popular.

Historically, Mongolians have never been farmers. The short summers and harsh climate made farming very difficult, and Mongolians have long believed that meat was the best food. They had a traditional saying, "Meat for men, leaves for animals." To balance their diet, they gathered berries that grew wild in the forests. Today farmers grow wheat, barley, and hardy vegetables, such as carrots,

Fresh fruit is a rare treat for Mongolian people, available only in the few warm weeks of summer. This boy is relishing some wild strawberries he has found.

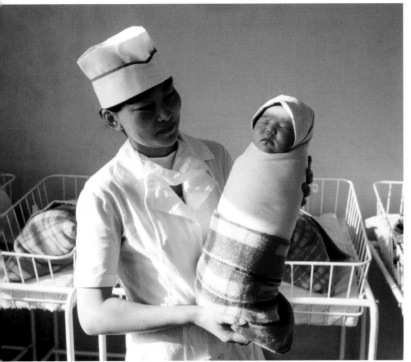

Mongolians rely on traditional and modern medicine. This nurse, in a modern hospital, smiles at the baby she has wrapped in the traditional way.

Health and Education

Mongolia's harsh environment causes various health problems. In freezing winters there is the danger of frostbite and hypothermia. In cities air pollution leads to skin irritations and chest complaints; in the countryside polluted water causes serious diseases, including cholera.

Livestock often carries brucellosis, which can be passed to humans and causes long-term fever and weakness. Marmots carry bubonic plague. Untreated, this kills most of its victims, and it can spread rapidly in devastating epidemics. There are also outbreaks of meningitis, which is often fatal. Packs of stray dogs can be infected with rabies, which kills all its victims unless they are promptly treated. Alcohol abuse is also a widespread problem.

During the communist era the Mongolian government greatly improved health care, training doctors and nurses and building free hospitals in towns and spas at natural hot springs. It set up clinics in the countryside and sent health education teams to nomad camps. As a result, Mongolians' life expectancy rose to about sixty-two years for men and sixty-seven years for women.

Since the end of communist rule, there has been less money for health care, and there are now fewer doctors, nurses, and life-saving medicines. Mongolians are returning to traditional medical treatments, based on animal or plant extracts, shamanistic rituals, or Buddhist prayers. The government elected in 2000 listed health and welfare as two of its main concerns.

Mongolians are among the best-educated people in Asia. Almost all adults can read and write. The state provides free education for children aged seven to seventeen, and there are both state and private universities. Nomadic children study in boarding schools for most of the year, returning home for a short mid-winter break and a three-month vacation in summertime. For nomadic adults, there are classes transmitted by radio.

However, educational standards in Mongolia have recently started to decline. As the nation becomes poorer, teenagers are dropping out of school to find work. Many older students do not go to universities because they cannot afford living expenses or tuition fees.

Arts and Sports

Traditional Mongolian arts and crafts were designed either to be portable, fitting in with the nomadic lifestyle, or to adorn Buddhist monasteries and temples. Nomad arts include clothes, jewelry, rugs, and woven bags. Religious art includes statues

The Three Main Sports

The three main sports, archery, horse racing, and wrestling, all have links with Mongolia's nomadic warrior past and are still very popular today.

In archery contests participants dressed in national costume shoot with curved Mongolian bows at ring-shaped targets 200 or 250 feet (60 or 75 meters) away. Horse racing can be dangerous, since jockeys, between five and thirteen years old, ride chaotically across rough countryside. In wrestling bouts huge contestants try to force each other to the ground. No holds are barred. Before each match wrestlers act out a traditional eagle dance as a sign of respect for each other's strength and bravery.

Competitors in an archery contest held during Naadam, the popular three-day Mongolian festival. Mongolian bows are small, but their double-curve shape makes them very powerful.

of Buddhist holy people, *tsam* (SAHM: masked dances on the Buddha's birthday), and *tangkas* (TAHNG-kuhs: sacred scroll-paintings used to help meditation). Traditional music played on the *morin khuur* (MOE-rihn KOOR: fiddle) is often about nomadic life. Songs in Mongolia's *khoomi* (KOO-mee) style, in which singers produce two tones at once, are also very popular, although young people like to listen to local Mongolian bands and international rock groups.

Crowds often flock to watch open-air sports competitions, especially at festival times. Winners receive large cash prizes and public acclaim. In towns and cities crowds enjoy watching soccer and basketball matches.

Mongolians are proud of their cultural heritage. These singers and musicians have dressed in magnificent costumes to perform traditional works.

MYANMAR

MYANMAR IS A TROPICAL LAND lying between the Indian subcontinent and Southeast Asia. It has a long coastline on the Indian Ocean.

Central Myanmar is formed by the basin of the Irrawaddy and Chindwin Rivers. A delta region advances into the Indian Ocean, dividing the Bay of Bengal from the Andaman Sea. Around the central lowlands the land rises to hill country, plateaus, and mountains, reaching 19,290 feet (5,880 meters) at Mount Hkakabo in the far north of the country.

Thousands of pilgrims, such as these two girls, take part in the three-day festival held each year at the Ananda Temple in Bagan, marking the full moon of the month of Pyatho.

Gold, Jade, and Elephants

The earliest settlers of the Myanmar (MYAN-mahr) coast may have been hunter-gatherers related to today's Andaman islanders. Many people migrated to the basin of the Irrawaddy (ihr-uh-WAH-dee) River, which is flanked by forested hills, to escape Southeast Asian wars or the ever-expanding Chinese (see CHINA) empire to the north. They found refuge in Myanmar's hills and rain forests, fertile land for farming in its river valleys and plains, and rich trading opportunities around the Bay of Bengal. Settlements were already developing in central Myanmar more than 4,500 years ago.

The most important of early migrants into the region were the Mon (MAWN). Probably originating from southwestern China, the Mon (related to the Khmer of Cambodia) had already settled large areas of Thailand (see THAILAND). The Mon advanced southward down the Irrawaddy, clearing rain forest and cultivating rice. They founded a series of independent city-states, each ruled by a king. Trading contacts with India (see INDIA) brought the first Buddhist missionaries to the region in the 200s B.C.E.

Migrations from Yunnan (Yoo-NAHN), in southwestern China, and the Tibetan plateau led to the arrival of new immigrants, speakers of Tibeto-Burman languages. Many of these moved into northern regions around the Irrawaddy basin. Collectively they were known as the Pyu (PYOO). They were established in the region by about 160 B.C.E. and governed by tribal assemblies.

FACTS AND FIGURES

Official name: *Union of Myanmar*

Status: *Independent state*

Capital: *Yangon*

Major towns: *Mandalay, Moulmein, Bago, Bassein, Sittwe, Taunggyi, Monywa*

Area: *261,789 square miles (678,034 square kilometers)*

Population: *49,500,000*

Population density: *189 per square mile (73 per square kilometer)*

Peoples: *68 percent Burman; 9 percent Shan; 7 percent Karen; 4 percent Rakhine; 3 percent Chinese; 2 percent Mon; 2 percent Indian and Bengali; 5 percent other, including Achang, Akha, Chin, Danaw, Hani, Hmong, Kachin, Kayah, Lahu, Lashi, Maru, Parauk, and Vo*

Official language: *Burmese*

Currency: *Kyat*

National days: *Independence Day (January 4); Union Day (February 12)*

Country's name: *Myanmar was known as Burma (named after the Burman people) until 1989. The local name for Burma had always been Myanma, and in 1989 the government adopted the spelling Myanmar as the official English version. The term Burma is still widely used in and outside the country.*

Developing a civilized and prosperous society, rich in gold, jade, pearls, and elephants, they traded with China and India and built cities. The Pyu were at the height of their power in the 400s C.E.

Time line:	Mon city-states founded; Buddhism arrives from India	Pyu settle in northern regions	Thai invasion causes the collapse of Pyu power
	200s B.C.E.	**160 B.C.E.**	**832**

CLIMATE

Myanmar has a generally hot and humid climate, affected by Indian Ocean winds. The southwest monsoon brings torrential rains from June to September. Even the winters are warm, except in highland regions.

	Yangon	Sittwe	Mandalay
Average January temperature:	*77°F (25°C)*	*70°F (21°C)*	*68°F (20°C)*
Average July temperature:	*80°F (27°C)*	*81°F (27°C)*	*85°F (29°C)*
Average annual precipitation:	*104 in. (264 cm)*	*206 in. (523 cm)*	*33 in. (84 cm)*

The Age of Bagan

After an attack from Thailand in 832, the Pyu states were weakened. They were largely absorbed into the realm of the Burmans (BER-muhnz), later migrants who had become the most numerous and powerful of all the Tibeto-Burman peoples living in Myanmar. In 849 the Burmans built a new walled city, called Bagan (buh-GAHN), or Pagan, 300 miles (480 kilometers) upstream from the mouth of the Irrawaddy. The Mon still occupied large areas of Myanmar. At about this time the center of Mon power moved northward from the city of Thaton (thuh-TAWN) to a new capital at Bago (BAH-goe), or Pegu.

Anawrahta, a ruler of Bagan who came to the throne in 1044, created the first Myanmar state, with boundaries similar to those of Myanmar today. He defeated the Mon ruler, Manuha, and set Mon captives to work building a series of splendid Buddhist temples and shrines around Bago. From this period onward the Burmans were heavily influenced by Mon culture.

To the east Anawrahta temporarily defeated the Shan (SHAHN) or Tai people, while to the west he became overlord of the Rakhine (rah-KEEN) kingdom on the Bay of Bengal, a region that had experienced Indian and then Pyu settlement. Anawrahta was killed by a wild buffalo in 1077.

Bagan rule was a golden age in the history of Myanmar. However, in the thirteenth century vast areas of Asia were conquered by Mongols, fierce warriors from the steppe grasslands of central Asia. They invaded northern China and founded a new dynasty of emperors, known as the Yuan. By 1279 they had conquered all of southern China too, triggering another exodus of peoples into Southeast Asia. Mongol-Chinese armies moved onward into Myanmar, and by 1287 they had overrun the country. The mayhem they created resulted in the downfall of the Bagan kingdom.

Founding of Bagan by the Burmans; the Mon capital moves to Bago	Anawrahta ascends the throne of Bagan	Mongol-Chinese armies move into Myanmar; downfall of Bagan kingdom
849	**1044**	**1287**

The City of Temples

The Burman king Anawrahta converted to Buddhism in 1056. In 1057 a triumphal procession of thirty-two elephants brought the Buddhist scriptures of the defeated Mon people back to Bagan. The new religious fervor of the Burmans was made clear by frenzied temple building on the plains around Bagan. Today these remain one of the most impressive archaeological sites in Southeast Asia, covering 16 square miles (41 square kilometers) and including the discovered remains of 2,217 temples, shrines, libraries, and monasteries. There are also more than a thousand brick mounds. Bagan has been damaged over the ages by Mongol invaders, by looters, by European explorers, and by earthquakes. Even so, an astonishing number of temples survive in all their splendor. They include beautiful wall paintings, sculptures, wood carvings, ceramic tiles, and plasterwork.

The ruined temples of Bagan stand mysteriously in the light of dawn. There are said to have been four thousand temples standing on this site at one time.

Mon, Shan, and Burmans

The following two hundred years saw continual warfare among small states in the Myanmar region. The Mon and Shan states expanded steadily until at last the Burman rulers of a city-state called Toungoo (TAWN-goo) succeeded in stamping their authority on the whole region. From the late 1400s throughout the 1500s, Mon cities were conquered by Toungoo. Toungoo rulers also fought long wars with Thailand until 1592.

Burman power eventually went into decline. The Shan founded a new kingdom called Inwa (IHN-wuh) in 1636, and the fortunes of the Mon also improved. They rose up against Burman rule in the 1740s.

Rise of the Burman state of Toungoo	Inwa becomes chief city of the Shan	Mon army occupies Inwa; European powers in southern Asia
1486	1636	1752

Bago prospered, and in 1752 the Mon captured Inwa as well. There was a fierce Burman reaction, led by an official from Shwebo called Alaungpaya. He founded a new ruling dynasty, captured Inwa and Bago, and moved the Burman capital to the seaport of Yangon (yahn-GAWN), previously called Rangoon.

Thai and British Wars

Around 1752 European powers were becoming involved in southern Asia. The Burmans were favored by the British, and the Mon by the French. From 1757 onward the British East India Company effectively ruled Bengal from its base at Kolkata (Calcutta, in India). The Company was a commercial corporation, but it had its own army and warships and the formidable backing of the British government.

The Burmans now began to expand their rule once more. In 1767 they sent soldiers into Thailand to destroy the then capital, Ayutthaya. However, when King Bodawpaya (ruled 1782–1819) annexed the Rakhine state, which bordered Bengal, the Burmans went too for the British. There were frontier quarrels and trading disputes, resulting in a war that lasted from 1824 to 1826. The defeated Burmans were forced to hand over not only Rakhine but also the southern Tenasserim (tuh-NAS-suh-rehm) region to the British. Further wars followed, after which the British gained Yangon and the rest of the south.

By 1858 rule over all of India and Bengal had passed to the British government. The Burman rulers tried to modernize what was

A Burman noblewoman poses for a formal photograph around 1900, during the period of British rule. She is accompanied by her servant.

left of their country. They even founded a new capital at Mandalay (man-duh-LAE). However, a trade dispute led to more warfare between them and the British. As a result, in 1886, all of Myanmar became a province of British India.

As colonial masters, the British increased rice cultivation and felled teak, a valuable hardwood timber in the tropical rain forests. British and U.S.–owned oil companies profited from an increasingly valuable petroleum industry, and Chinese workers and storekeepers were encouraged to move in. However, many Burmans felt that they were now deprived of both power and wealth. They resented the fact that

Burman army destroys Thai capital of Ayutthaya	War with Britain; Myanmar loses Rakhine and Tenasserim	New capital at Mandalay
1767	**1824–1826**	**1858**

much of the administration was now carried out by Indian and Bengali officials and that the British allowed the hill peoples of Myanmar a degree of autonomy that was denied to the Burmans themselves.

From 1906 onward nationalist students and Buddhist monks fostered anti-British protests in a campaign for independence. They were met by oppression and jailed. The liberation movement reached a climax in the 1930s under the leadership of U Aung San (lived 1915–1947) and U Nu (lived 1907–1995). In 1936 Myanmar was made into a British colony in its own right, separate from India and with a measure of self-government.

Japan and Jungle Warfare

Further developments were halted by World War II (1939–1945), which devastated Myanmar more than any other country in Southeast Asia, causing long-

Allied troops transport goods across the Irrawaddy River in December 1944. World War II saw very large casualties amongst Allies, Japanese, and Burmese.

term damage to the economy. In 1942 Japanese troops, mobilized by a government intent on militarism and regional domination, overran most of Southeast Asia. As Japanese troops invaded Myanmar, the British retreated westward to Bengal, destroying crops, roads, and bridges as they withdrew. The Japanese were welcomed as liberators by many nationalists. Some of them joined a puppet government led by nationalist Ba Maw (lived 1893–1977).

For three years irregular warfare raged through Myanmar's rain forests, as British aircraft dropped special army units behind Japanese lines. British and U.S. troops maintained hazardous links with anti-Japanese forces in China, by air and by land, along a strip running into Yunnan, which became known as the "Burma Road."

In 1945 Burmese nationalists, led by U Aung San, changed sides and offered support to the Allies as they fought their way back into Myanmar, finally defeating the Japanese at the Battle of the Irrawaddy.

Myanmar becomes a province of British-ruled India	Start of nationalist agitation against British rule	Myanmar made a separate British colony
1886	**1906**	**1936**

Troubled Independence

After the war the nationalists pressed the British strongly for independence. U Aung San, leader of the Anti-Fascist People's Freedom League (AFPFL), promised self-determination to the minorities. A general election, held in April 1947, resulted in a landslide victory for U Aung San. Tragically, within a few months, he and five colleagues were assassinated, probably by a political rival. When independence finally arrived in January 1948, the new AFPFL prime minister was U Nu.

U Nu was reelected twice. The country took on a high international profile when a Burman diplomat called U Thant became Secretary-General of the United Nations Organization. He played an important role as peacemaker on the world stage between 1961 and 1971.

However, these were troubled times. Communists revolted against the government, and so did Karen (kuh-REHN) separatists in the southeast. In 1962 U Nu was overthrown in a military coup, led by General Ne Win, and jailed for four years. Ne Win centralized economic and political control, and in 1972 he created a civilian-style presidential government, but it was still repressive and a one-party state was declared in 1974.

The Democracy Movement

In 1988 pro-democracy uprisings and demonstrations were brutally suppressed by Ne Win, causing many deaths. A military government took power again

Daw Aung San Suu Kyi makes a speech in 1989. She won the general election the following year but was barred from power by the SLORC.

under General Saw Maung of the governing State Law and Order Council (SLORC), with the aging Ne Win remaining powerful in the background. Thousands of dissidents were arrested and sentenced to forced labor.

A general election was at last held in 1990, which was won by the National League for Democracy (NLD), led by U Nu and U Aung San's daughter, Daw Aung San Suu Kyi (born 1945). However, the government refused to acknowledge its defeat or concede power. In fact, they placed the NLD leaders under house arrest. There was persecution of opposition campaigners and also of ethnic minorities such as the Karen, the Kachin (kuh-CHIHN), and the Rohingya (roe-hihn-GYA).

Japanese invasion	Assassination of U Aung San	Independence; U Nu becomes prime minster	Military coup led by General Ne Win
1942	1947	1948	1962

The suppression of democracy and human-rights abuses were condemned internationally. In 1991 Daw Aung San Suu Kyi was awarded the Nobel Peace Prize. Famous around the world, with overwhelming support in her own country, she remained under arrest until 1995. In 1997 the SLORC government was replaced by a State Peace and Development Council (SPDC). However, its leadership was made up of the same people, and political repression continued. Daw Aung San Suu Kyi was under house arrest again from 2000 to 2002.

In 2003 the SPDC announced that it would restore democracy. However, Daw Aung San Suu Kyi was arrested yet again and detained at a secret location. There

A young boy grins as he peers through the window of a Burmese house. One-third of the population is made up of children below the age of fifteen.

were reports that she was on hunger strike in protest, and the United Nations warned that the Myanmar government alone would be held responsible for her welfare.

The Burman People

Citizens of Myanmar are called Burmese, while the majority ethnic group is known as Burmans. The Burmans account for about 68 percent of the population. They are widely spread across the country, but most live in the densely populated central lowlands around the Irrawaddy River.

Western dress such as shirts, pants, T-shirts, jeans, and skirts are seen in the cities, but nine out of ten men and women in both town and country tend to wear a *longyi* (LAWNG-yee), a colored, patterned piece of cloth worn around the waist. It is a practical garment, which can be tucked

Brutal repression of pro-democracy protestors	Rulers refuse to acknowledge election victory of Daw Aung San Suu Kyi	Daw Aung San Suu Kyi under house arrest; government promises a return to democracy
1988	**1990**	**2003**

A large family group stands outside their home in Mandalay, in central Myanmar. The city of about 800,000 remains at the heart of the Burman culture.

up to allow greater movement for, say, manual labor. The male version is worn ankle length; the female version can be shorter. The longyi may be worn with a shirt, blouse, or a tailored short jacket. Men may tie a strip of cloth around their head or wear a small turban for formal occasions. Sandals are worn on the feet but are taken off in the home and at Buddhist temples.

In Burman society respect is shown to older people and to those of a high social status. The extended family of grandparents, aunts, uncles, and cousins plays an important part in family life. Women have often held power in the

history of Myanmar, and they play an important part in most Burman communities. They have equal status before the law, but they suffer from low pay compared with men and from lack of status within the local Buddhist tradition.

Hill and Coastal Peoples

Myanmar is home to many different peoples: some groups numbering only several hundred, others reaching hundreds of thousands or even millions. In a nation the size of Texas, there are 135 officially recognized minorities referred to as "national races" and 107 different languages. The minorities often vary from the Burmans in their religious beliefs, farming practices, social organization, and in their dress. Many wear variants of the longyi, some wear wide pants, and some have distinctive jewelry, headdresses, or turbans.

This ethnic diversity offers a rich mixture of cultures, but it has also been at the root of political tensions throughout the history of the region. Several minorities currently wage armed campaigns against central government and wish to withdraw from Myanmar. Human-rights organizations accuse the government of oppressing minorities. Many hill peoples have fled persecution by the army, crossing into Thailand as refugees.

The chief minorities have their own states, although this does not reflect significant devolution of centralized power. The Mon State has its capital at Moulmein (mool-MAHN). After centuries of mingling with the Burmans, the Mon make up only 2 percent of all Burmese, but they remain proud of their history and culture.

The Shan ethnic group, which is also found in Assam (India), China, Thailand, and Laos, form Myanmar's largest minority, making up about 9 percent of the national population. They live mostly around the plateaus and valleys of Shan State, around the Salween (SAHL-ween) River in the east of the country. Depending on the local terrain, they grow rice, tea, coffee, fruit, or potatoes.

The Karen are also skilled farmers, living in Karen State along the mountainous border with Thailand. They grow rice by dry cultivation, mostly for consumption within their own villages. There are various subgroups of Karen, speaking languages and dialects of the Tibeto-Burman family. There is great tension between the Karen and the central government. During British rule many Karen became officials or trained as teachers or doctors, and ever since 1948, they have campaigned for their own independence.

Remote and mountainous Kayah State is home to the hill farming Kayah (KIE-uh). They belong to a completely different ethnic group than the Karen, but are also called Red Karen (or Karenni), because of

Words, Writing, and Palm Leaves

The language of the Burmans is called Burmese and belongs to the Tibeto-Burman language family. The official language of Myanmar, it has five distinct dialects and is spoken as a second language by several million members of the minorities. The Burmese alphabet, known as ca-lonh (cuh-LAWN: "round-hand"), dates back to the 1100s, when it was adapted from the script used by the Mon people. Traditionally people used palm leaves to write on, which is said to have determined the rounded shape of the letters.

min-gala-ba (mihn-GAH-luh-buh)	hello
ce-zu-beh (CHE-roo-buh)	thank you
houq-keh (HOO-keh)	yes
mahouq-pa'bu (muh-HOOK-pah-boo)	no
tiq, hniq, thoun, le, nga (TEEK, NEEK, THOON, LEH, uhn-GAH)	one, two, three, four, five
ywa (uh-WAH)	village
pahto (PAH-toe)	temple
paya (PIE-uh)	pagoda (shrine)

Rings of Brass

The Ka-Kaung (kuh-KAWNG), or Padaung, are a people of the Karen ethnic group who live on the Thai border. In the past they have long fascinated outsiders because of the way in which some of their women wear neck rings, which, added to over the years, may reach a height of 10 in. (25 cm). These rings are made of rattan (a type of cane) covered in brass and can weigh up to 11 pounds (5 kilograms). This necklace deforms the body, pushing down the collarbone and ribs while forcing the chin upward, to give the impression of a long neck. Today the practice is largely dying out among younger women in Myanmar.

Some Ka-Kaung women still wear brass neck rings. An ancient myth claims that their people are descended from a long-necked dragon.

the scarlet skirts worn by their women. They speak a Tibeto-Burman language, but their neighbors along the Thai border are a group of peoples known as the Palaung (puh-LAWNG), whose language belongs to the Mon-Khmer family of Southeast Asia.

The Kachin, or Jingpho, are another Tibeto-Burman hill people, living in scattered villages in the far north, along the Chinese and Indian borders. They live by herding and by growing rice, millet, and corn. Traditional women's clothing includes finely woven skirts and blouses decorated with silver medallions.

The Chin (CHIHN) are a hill people living in the northwestern Chin State and in the Arakan Yoma (ah-ruh-KAHN YOE-muh) Mountains. They are related to groups living in Bangladesh and Assam. There are many subgroups within Myanmar, speaking various dialects and languages. Chin women traditionally tattooed their faces, but this custom is no longer practiced.

The Intha people, a small minority living on islands in Inle Lake, build thatched houses on tall stilts. They speak a dialect of the Burmese language.

The beautiful Shwedagon Paya in Yangon, with its golden roofs and shrines, has become a symbol of the Burmese nation as a whole.

Minority peoples live at different altitudes. Their villages are mostly made of bamboo or hardwood timbers and are thatched with straw or leaves. They may be raised on stilts to avoid monsoon floods or they may be at ground level with beaten earth floors.

The Rakhine, or Arakanese, of the western coast make up about 4 percent of the national population. Their language is Tibeto-Burman, and they are descended from Pyu and Bengali colonizers. Myanmar also has a population of Chinese, Bengali, and Indian descent, together making up about 5 percent of the national population.

Acts of Faith

About nine out of ten Burmese are Buddhists. Buddhism originated in northern India about 2,500 years ago. Its founder, the Buddha, also known as the Enlightened One, taught of the ways in which people can find relief from daily suffering through their actions. He believed that all creatures are reborn to live through many lifetimes before finally achieving an enlightened state, or nirvana.

In Myanmar most Buddhists follow the Theravada form of Buddhism, which is also practiced in Thailand, Laos, Cambodia, and Sri Lanka. Theravada places great importance on being a monk and following strictly the original teachings of the Buddha. Many people take vows of poverty and become monks (wearing dark red robes) or nuns (wearing light red robes). Supporting monks or helping to maintain a temple are seen as acts of merit, deeds that will help one achieve enlightenment.

Myanmar has countless Buddhist holy places. Known as *paya* (PIE-uh), they include solid dome-shaped shrines (stupas), often housing sacred relics, and temple buildings. These are not places of communal worship, but are built for meditation, pilgrimage, or acts of merit. Holiest and most spectacular of all is Shwedagon (shwa-DAWNG) Paya in Yangon. The site was originally built by the Mon, perhaps 1,500 years ago, and has been constantly renewed and revered over the ages. Outside Shwedagon pilgrims pay to release caged doves, a symbol of the respect shown by Buddhists to all living creatures.

Myanmar's oldest religious tradition is that of animism, or the worship of nature spirits called *nat* (NAHT), which are believed to control human fate. Animism is still practiced among many of the hill peoples, and in mainstream society animism very often underlies a faith in Buddhism. Offerings are made to the nat at the shrines that guard homes or temples. Special musical festivals are held where the nat are summoned by a shaman. The shaman is either a woman or a man dressed as a woman.

Young boys wear the robes of a monk as they line up for a drink in Yangon. Theravada Buddhism encourages everyone to experience the life of a monk.

The Boy Monks

The most important ceremony of boyhood in Myanmar is Shinpyu *(SHIMP-yoo), held around March each year. It starts with music and a grand feast, attended by Buddhist monks, friends, and family. A young boy is dressed up as a prince, and as happened with the Buddha himself, his clothes are then cast aside. The boy's head is shaved, and he is dressed in the simple robes of a monk. He is then handed a begging bowl, like that of a monk asking for alms, and continues on to take a solemn oath: "I seek the refuge of the Buddha . . . the Law . . . the Order of Monks." After this he goes to spend the night in a monastery, as a temporary monk. Short periods of life as a monk are repeated in boyhood and sometimes later in life. The experience serves to teach young people about the Buddhist faith.*

Two men share a joke as they prepare seafood in Setse, a beach resort on the south coast that is famous for its shellfish.

From the 1800s onward, Baptist and Roman Catholic missionaries from North America and Europe converted some animists to Christianity, and Christianity is still strong among the Karen, the Kachin, and the Chin peoples. The center of Islam in Myanmar is Rakhine State. Many people of Indian descent are Hindus, and their temples can be seen in Yangon.

Rice, Curry, and Seafood Paste

At mealtimes in the home most families eat around a low table, sitting on mats. Fingers are generally used instead of utensils, but forks, spoons, and chopsticks may be used. The diet is a healthy one, based on the staple food of rice (boiled, fried, or with coconut) or noodles (made from wheat or rice). These are normally served with dishes of curried vegetables, such as cabbage, carrot, radish, onion, and corn, or with curried lamb, chicken, or prawns. Food may be flavored with garlic, ginger, turmeric (a yellow spice made from a plant of the same name), coriander, or pastes and salty sauces made from dried seafood.

Myanmar offers a wealth of fresh tropical fruits, including mangoes,

A popular pavement café offers noodles to hungry customers on a busy street in central Yangon. The capital offers a wide range of Burmese, Indian, Chinese, and Western foods.

papayas, pineapples, watermelons, and citrus fruits such as limes. Durian is a Southeast Asian specialty. It is a large fruit covered in a spiky skin, containing a creamy pulp. People find it delicious, but outsiders are often put off by its smell, which is decidedly rotten.

Teahouses are found on many streets, serving tea hot, sweet, and milky, along with all sorts of pastries and snacks. A sweet beverage made from palm juice is also very popular.

Farms, Rain Forests, and Fishing

Myanmar is a land of farmers, with seven out of ten workers employed on the land. About 15 percent of the land area is under cultivation. Monsoon flooding and drought are common problems, and farming depends on irrigation in some regions. In some areas of hill country, the traditional method of farming is to clear forest and then allow it to grow back once the soil has been exhausted. This method is called slash-and-burn agriculture.

The chief crop is rice, grown in the rich soil of the monsoon-drenched Irrawaddy basin, as well as in marginal highland regions. Other crops include sugarcane, peanuts, beans and pulses (such as lentils), corn, and tobacco (traditionally smoked in large cigars). Rubber trees are also grown on plantations.

Farming is largely unmechanized, with much of the hard work being done by lumbering water buffalo rather than tractors. Farming villages vary from one region to another, but are mostly made up of simple houses of bamboo and thatch, often built on timber stilts in order to keep dry in the rainy season. After a hard day's work, families sit out on their house's long porch to gossip, exchange news, and tell stories.

Many country people are very poor and in remote areas make money by cultivating poppies, which are processed for the illegal international trade as opium and heroin. Eastern Myanmar and cross-border regions of Thailand and Laos became known as "The Golden Triangle" in the 1970s and 1980s, as regional warlords and armies

---

Dishes of Myanmar

Myanmar's cooking has been influenced by that of neighboring Thailand, China, and Bangladesh. With the exception of the Shan, most Burmese prefer mild curries. Myanmar's Muslims eat no pork; its Hindus, and many of its Buddhists, eat no beef; while other Buddhists eat mostly vegetarian or fish dishes.

- **Kyay-o** *(CHIE-oe) is made of minced pork, quail eggs, green mustard leaves, and noodles.*

- **Mohinga** *(moe-hihng-GUH) is a dish of fine noodles served in a fish sauce.*

- **Thouq** *(THOOK) are fresh vegetable or fruit salads seasoned with spices, chilies, and peanuts, often served with rice.*

- **Oun-no-hkauq-sweh** *(oo-noe-KAWK-sweh) is chicken in a coconut sauce served with noodles.*

- **Nga-baun-douq** *(uhn-gah-bawn-DOOK) is fish steamed in banana leaves.*

- **Freshwater fish** *dishes include carp, catfish, and eel.*

- **Hnetpyaw-kyaw** *(nehp-YAWK-yaw) are bananas fried in a rice flour batter.*

Working with Elephants

The Asian elephant is the largest animal ever to be tamed. It has been used for hauling heavy goods for thousands of years. In most of Southeast Asia the use of elephants in the logging industry is in decline, but the state-owned Myanmar Timber Enterprises still has 4,500 working elephants at its lumber camps. They are used to push, haul, and stack teak logs, which may each weigh up to 1.3 tons (1.2 metric tonnes).

The elephant handler, or u-zi (OO-ZEE), must get to know and trust each animal individually, since this can be dangerous work in unskilled hands. Learning to be a handler takes many years, and there are plenty of commands, movements, and pressure points for both animal and human to learn. Each day the handler must fit the thick protective saddle and other tackle and then perch on top of the elephant's massive neck. He is responsible for watering the elephant and feeding it (with rice). By night the elephant is allowed to roam the rain forest, but its legs are tied in a way that prevents it from going too far away.

A working elephant hauls a log through the river in a forested area near Toungoo. Rain forests and elephants are both in decline across Southeast Asia.

from rebel minorities sought to profit from drug smuggling. By 2002 the production of drugs was falling considerably, but even so, Myanmar was still the world's second biggest producer of illegal opium.

Over 50 percent of Myanmar is forested, and large areas of land are taken up by valuable tropical hardwood species, such as teak, pyinkado, and padauk. These are logged commercially and account for over 20 percent of the country's exports. With an acute concern about deforestation across Southeast Asia, there have been worries about illegal logging in Myanmar. The

A fisher of the Intha people poles a boat across the still waters of Inle Lake, carrying a large bamboo-framed net used for catching carp.

depletion of rain forest is made worse by the spread of the population into conservation areas, by slash-and-burn farming, and by the use of wood as a domestic fuel. Steps are now being taken to manage rain forests and plant new trees.

Fish forms a major part of the Burmese diet, and 25 percent of the catch is netted in lakes and rivers. Indian Ocean waters are rich in species, but competition is fierce and they are heavily fished. The development of modern fishing ports threatens coastal environments, which are currently protected from flooding by the tangled roots of mangrove swamps. Shrimp farming and fish farming are increasingly important, and pearls are cultivated too.

Resources and Industry

Myanmar is rich in mineral resources, including natural gas, petroleum, gemstones, coal, tungsten, copper, zinc, lead, and silver. Its power stations use 44 percent fossil fuels (coal, gas, or oil) for generation and 56 percent hydroelectric power. Myanmar trades with China, Taiwan, Japan, the United States, India, and several countries in Southeast Asia.

The country's poverty is largely the result of economic mismanagement and corruption by its military rulers from the 1960s onward. After 1988 economic reforms were made, reducing public ownership. There has been some improvement in the economy, and Myanmar is no longer near the bottom of the world poverty list. Even so, about one-fourth of the Burmese population is still thought to live below the poverty line, and they face rising prices for basic purchases. The country's true economic position is hard to evaluate because there is a large amount of illegal or unregistered international trade and because official statistics are hard to come by. The suppression of democracy and the continuing uncertainty as a result of political unrest have deterred foreign investment.

About 7 percent of the labor force is industrial workers. Factories and mills process timber, metal ores, and foods and produce fertilizers, building materials, knitwear, textiles, and finished garments. Industrial pollution is a problem. Twenty-three percent of workers are employed in services, such as tourism, catering, education, or medicine.

Transportation and communications in Myanmar are in need of development. Only 12 percent of Myanmar's 17,500 miles (28,000 kilometers) of road have paved, all-weather surfaces. Landslides cause

Streets of Yangon

Only 27 percent of the population lives in towns, and about 4 million of those live in Yangon. Capital of Myanmar, it is a center of communications, transportation, business, and trade as well as being the country's chief port. It is built on the Yangon River, 21 miles (34 kilometers) from the ocean. Yangon is full of a variety of modern buildings made of concrete and glass alongside old British colonial buildings, hotels, churches, mosques, and temples, most notably the golden Shwedagon Paya. The streets are busy with pickup trucks, buses, taxi cabs, bicycles, carts, and pedal-powered

pedicabs (a tricycle with a seat at the back for passengers). The city is served by trains and buses, and the river is plied by small wooden boats, or sampans, and by ferries. Yangon's busy markets represent the most vibrant side of the city, selling rolls of cloth, tropical fruit and vegetables, fish, handicrafts, and household goods. The city is rapidly modernizing, but it still has a leisurely old-world atmosphere, with leafy public gardens offering peace and shade.

The Yangon skyline—colonial, traditional, and modern— takes in many different styles of architecture, amidst tropical palms and busy streets.

Spools of colorful yarn will be used to weave longyis at this workshop in Meiktila, a lakeside town to the east of Bagan.

airstrips in remote areas and eight airports with paved runways. The national carrier, Myanmar Airways, flies to Bangkok, in Thailand, and Singapore.

The country has few telephone landlines, and a small, if rapidly growing, number of cell phones may be seen on the streets of Yangon. Few people own personal computers, and Internet access is restricted by the government to its own civil service, tourism connections, and major business users.

problems in the rainy season, and Myanmar is an earthquake zone, which is another natural hazard. There are about 2,500 miles (4,000 kilometers) of rail track, and many goods are carried by boat or ship on the country's rivers and waterways. There are

Boats are a way of life on Myanmar's lakes, rivers, and coasts. They are used for fishing, transportation, as market stalls, and as homes.

Schools and Hospitals

Myanmar has a long tradition of free education, provided by Buddhist monasteries, and this is still the case today. However, in addition to this, a state-run education system has been set up since independence in 1948. Most children attend elementary school, but attendance

High school girls stand in line, umbrellas raised against the hot sun. Although women play an important part in Burmese society, they have a lower literacy rate than men.

drops as they grow up. Tuition must be paid from senior high school level onward, and there is a desperate shortage of properly trained teachers. There are nine universities and over twenty colleges of further education. The government claims that 89 percent of males and 78 percent of females over fifteen can read and write. The real figures are believed to be far lower, although book reading is a popular pastime.

There is a chronic shortage of doctors in Myanmar and, therefore, serious problems with health care. Life expectancy at birth is only fifty-four for men and fifty-nine for women. These figures compare with seventy and seventy-five in neighboring Thailand. Dangerous illnesses include malaria and dengue fever (both carried by mosquitoes). Poor sanitation and water supply lead to dysentery and typhoid.

Many Burmese place their faith in traditional folk medicines, purchased in the marketplace and made up of herbs, leaves, bark, roots, and parts of animals, including many of the country's venomous snakes.

Journalists and Writers

The years of military government and state control have seen censorship and propaganda become normal in Myanmar's communications media. There are four national daily newspapers in Burmese and one, the *New Light of Myanmar*, in English. There are also many weeklies and magazines. Radio and television are state owned, but many people listen to broadcasts from overseas networks.

Puppets Come to Life

One of Myanmar's greatest art forms is the marionette (stringed puppet) theater. This tradition is believed to have originated in India and China, but the Burmese made it their own. The first puppetry probably dates from the Bagan period, but the high point was reached in the 1700s and 1800s, when the puppets were permitted much greater license to mock or criticize than human actors would ever have been allowed. Today the marionette tradition is sadly in decline, often depending upon tourist shows and manufactured souvenirs.

Burmese puppets stand around 3 feet (1 meter) high and move to musical accompaniment. They are carved from wood, painted, and then dressed in fine costumes. The shows are based on tales from the life of the Buddha or on much-loved legends. They include a number of stock characters, such as the white horse, the monkey, ogres, the wizard, the female shaman, the court jester, the king, queen, prince, and princess.

These marionettes are about 100 years old and date from the golden age of Burmese puppetry. The puppets are made to dance and reenact ancient tales.

Satellite television is also opening Myanmar up to the outside world.

The royal court of Myanmar was the center of literature and the arts until British rule. The earliest surviving texts are Buddhist scriptures, over nine hundred years old. Poetry thrived, but the depth and variety of Burmese literature cannot match that of neighboring Bengal or China. Printing did not arrive in Myanmar until the nineteenth century. Myanmar inspired British writers, from Rudyard Kipling (1865–1936, author of *The Jungle Book*), whose popular poem *Mandalay* was an affectionate look at Myanmar through the eyes of a common soldier, to George Orwell (1903–1950, author of *Animal Farm*), who criticized British rule in *Burmese Days*.

The Arts and Crafts

Myanmar's liveliest performances are popular opera shows, which take place at festivals and private celebrations. They are a mixture of words, music, and dance, often with satirical comedy routines. Classical Burmese dance originated at the royal court and was influenced by Thai dance styles of the 1700s. Single dancers act out a variety of stylized movements and gestures.

At the end of the wet season in September or October, boat races and rowing festivals are held all over Myanmar. Traditional music is played on board this boat near Mandalay.

Myanmar's classical music was influenced by that of Thailand and is very different from Western music. Musicians play by ear rather than by reading notes from a sheet. Their instruments include tuned drums, gongs, cymbals, the *se* (SAE: a brass percussion instrument), the *wa* (WAH: bamboo clappers), flutes, and xylophones. Folk music is often based on simple country songs, performed without instruments. Myanmar has a lively modern music scene, heavily influenced by Western pop styles.

Burmese craftwork has a history dating back to the construction of the country's classical Buddhist temples and palaces, which were adorned with beautifully carved wood, paintings, and sculptures. Today's jewelers work with locally mined jade, rubies, and sapphires. Lacquerware is made by coating boxes, bowls, tables, and screens with layers of a special sap taken from a type of tropical tree. It dries to become hard, tough, and shiny.

Myanmar's textile skills may be seen in the weaving of the longyi, and many of the finest quality cloths and designs are created by minority peoples. Hill peoples such as the Akha (AH-kuh), Chin, and Karen produce embroidered jackets or blouses. The *kalaga* (kuh-luh-GAH), or temple cloth, is a tapestry with a pattern in raised cotton padding, embroidered in silver thread, and decorated with sequins and studs. Its design may be based on tales from the Buddha's life, nat spirits, or elephants.

Kicking and Jumping

Soccer is one of Myanmar's most popular sports, and it is played in every town. Skills are no doubt improved by practicing Myanmar's oldest sport, *chinlon* (CHIHN-lawn). This goes back to the Pyu era but was not formalized as a sport until the twentieth century. It is sometimes played at festivals with musical accompaniment. The ball, about 4 inches (10 centimeters) in diameter, is made of rattan wickerwork. The players' aim is to keep the ball in the air for as long as possible by a series of prescribed movements that make use of the feet, knees, calves, head, shoulders, and elbows—basically anything except the hands. At a formal game six players stand in a circle and score points for each successful move. An alternative version is to play the game as volleyball, over a net but again without using hands. Chinlon has recently become popular with women as well as men.

Thai kickboxing is well known internationally as a martial art. Burmese kickboxing, which originally came from Thailand, is less famous. However, it is hugely popular and even more violent. The opponents in the ring can kick, punch, leap, and elbow each other. Musicians often play along during the contest to dramatize the action.

Another Myanmar martial art is called *bando* (BAHN-doe), also known as *thaing* (THANG). It is a combination of many self-defense and combat skills, originally practiced in eastern Asia, and uses techniques similar to those of karate, judo, and Chinese swordplay. During World War II the sport came under Japanese influence. An International Bando Association was founded in 1946.

Burmese Festivals

Myanmar's national days, Independence Day (January 4) and Union Day (February 12), are marked by public holidays, festivals, and fairs. Most of Myanmar's traditional and Buddhist festivals are determined by the phases of the Moon, so they do not fall on the same day each year.

Making a Splash

Myanmar's New Year arrives on the first day of Tagu *(tuh-GOO) month (usually in April). The weather is very hot, which is lucky, since the chief way of celebrating the day is to hurl water at strangers in the street. Soon everyone is soaked to the skin. This practice has been taking place for a long time, as far back as at the court of the Bagan kings.*

This three-day festival of fun is called Thingyan *(thihng-YAHN), which is believed to come from a Sanskrit (ancient Indian) word meaning "change." Water is a symbol of a fresh start in many religions. In Myanmar there is ceremonial hair washing of the elderly, as a mark of respect, and a cleansing of the statues in the temples. Special food is given to monks. Offerings of flowers are made to the nats or guardian spirits of the home. Thingyan is also a time for all sorts of fun and unruly behavior, and for once the girls are allowed to be just as wild as the boys.*

Among these are many regional and minority cultural traditions, as well as innumerable festivals associated with pagodas and temples. An example of the latter is a three-week festival held at the Phaung Daw U Paya (shrine) in Shan State in September and October. During this, gold-covered Buddhist statues are taken from the temple and carried in barges across Inle (IHN-law) Lake.

January's chief celebration is a big harvest festival across the nation. It is centered upon rice—or *htamane* (tuh-muh-NAE). Rice is cooked in huge quantities in every village and divided among the people. Around March comes the most important of all the pagoda festivals, the special day of Shwedagon Paya in Yangon. Religious ceremonies are held to commemorate a sacred relic, the eight hairs of the Buddha, which are said to be buried in a casket under a slab of gold at the heart of the temple. The festival is marked by dancing and drama, and the streets are lined with stalls selling food.

April or May is the time of the Buddha's birthday, which is marked at temples by the watering of sacred banyan trees (the Buddha is said to have achieved enlightenment under such a tree at Bodh Gayā, in India). The full moon of *Waso* (WAH-soe) month, around July, is Dhammasetkya (dah-muh-SEHK-yuh) Day, marking the start of a Buddhist holy season rather like that of the Christian Lent. The rainy season starts around this time, and people concentrate on religious matters. Some stop eating meat, and monks retreat to the monasteries to meditate.

Around the end of September there are boat races held on rivers and lakes around the country, an old royal tradition. The end of the rainy season and the end of the Buddhist "Lent" is marked by pilgrimages to holy sites and a beautiful festival of lights and lanterns. Kahtein Thingan (kuh-TAEN thihng-GAHN) is part of the religious

Glittering costumes, tiaras, and best clothes are a feature of the family processions marking a festival day at Yangon's famous Shwedagon Paya.

calendar, marked by donations of new robes, money, and offerings to monks. October and November bring another festival of lights and fireworks, celebrating the full moon in the month of *Tazaungmon* (tuh-zawng-MAWN). Myanmar's religious minorities follow their own religious festivals, with Christmas being celebrated by Christian Karen, Kachin, and Chin.

NEPAL

NEPAL IS A SMALL, LANDLOCKED COUNTRY IN THE HIMALAYAS.
It is one of the most mountainous countries in the world.

The great mountains of the Himalaya range stretch across Nepal's northern borders. The country has eight peaks over 26,000 feet (8,000 meters), including Mount Everest at 29,028 feet (8,848 meters) — the highest mountain peak in the world.

Nepal has three main geographic regions. In the south is the Terai, the northernmost limit of the Ganga River floodplain. It is an area of mostly low-lying, fertile land, where much of Nepal's important rice crop is grown. Central Nepal is made up of lower mountains and valleys and includes the Kathmandu Valley, the most heavily populated and heavily farmed region of Nepal. In the north are the High Himalayas. About one in ten of Nepal's population lives here.

Pokharā, in central Nepal, looking over the still waters of Lake Phewa to the Annapurna Range in the High Himalayas. In the middle is the beautiful Machapuchare, the "fishtail" mountain.

Early History

The first written references to Nepal (neh-PAHL) appear in different Indian sources, including the great Hindu epic, the *Mahabharata* (mah-huhb-RAH-tah). They refer to the Kiratis (kih-RAH-tees), a people of Mongoloid origin who came from the east in the seventh or eighth century B.C.E. The Kiratis established small settlements and were probably sheep farmers and wool

---

CLIMATE

Nepal's climate varies according to altitude. In the low-lying south the climate is subtropical and humid. Central Nepal has cool winters and warm summers, compared to the harsh winters and cool summers of the Himalayas. Most of Nepal's rain falls during the southwest monsoon (June–September), often resulting in violent storms, flooding, and landslides.

Kathmandu

Average January temperature:	*49°F (9°C)*
Average July temperature:	*75°F (24°C)*
Average annual precipitation:	*52 in. (132 cm)*

FACTS AND FIGURES

Official name: *Kingdom of Nepal*

Status: *Independent state*

Capital: *Kathmandu*

Major towns: *Bhaktapur, Patan, Pokharā, Biratnagar*

Area: *54,362 square miles (140,798 square kilometers)*

Population: *25,874,000*

Population density: *476 per square mile (184 per square kilometer)*

Peoples: *Three major ethnic groups: Tibeto-Nepalese; Indo-Nepalese; indigenous Nepalese*

Official language: *Nepali*

Currency: *Nepalese rupee*

National day: *Birthday of King Gyanendra (July 7)*

Country's name: *The origins of the name are uncertain. There is mention in early Chinese literature that Nepal means "the home of wool." This may come from the time of the Kiratis, who probably traded wool.*

---

traders. They were also the first rulers of the Kathmandu (kat-man-DOO) Valley.

During the Kirati period Buddhism began to spread in the Kathmandu Valley. Siddhartha Gautama (ca. 563–483 B.C.E.), who came to be known as the Buddha, was born at Lumbinī (luhm-BEE-nee) in southern Nepal, although he spent most of his life traveling and preaching in India (see INDIA). The Buddhist Indian Emperor Ashoka is said to have erected a stone pillar at the Buddha's birthplace.

The Licchavis, Thakuris, and Mallas

In the fourth century C.E. the Kirati rulers were overthrown by Rajput (RAHJ-poot) invaders from north India. They established the Licchavi (lih-CHAH-vee) dynasty and controlled the Kathmandu Valley for more than three hundred years, establishing the first true Nepali state.

Time line:	Kiratis establish settlements and become first rulers of the Kathmandu Valley	Rajput invaders from India establish the Licchavi dynasty; golden age in Nepal's history	First of the Thakuri kings comes to the throne; Nepal's "Dark Ages"
	7th or 8th century B.C.E.	**300s C.E.**	**600s**

Under the Licchavis, Buddhism declined and Hinduism became the dominant religion. The caste system (the Hindu system of organizing society into classes) was introduced. The Licchavi period was a golden time in Nepali art and culture. The kingdom prospered through extensive trade links with India, Tibet, and China.

In the seventh century the first of the Thakuri (tah-KOO-ree) kings came to the throne. The Thakuri period became known as the "Dark Ages;" there were invasions from an increasingly powerful Tibet, and there was frequent instability in the kingdom. Yet trade and settlements continued to grow in the Kathmandu Valley. In the tenth century the city of Kathmandu — then known as Kantipur (KAHN-tih-poor) — was founded.

The Malla (MAH-lah) dynasty began in the thirteenth century and continued until the eighteenth century. In the early years of the Mallas, the Muslim conquest of northern India spread conflict and upheaval into Nepal. In the early fourteenth century, a huge earthquake killed many thousands of people in the Kathmandu Valley, but the valley towns that became Kathmandu, Patan (puh-TAHN), and Bhaktapur (BAHK-tuh-poor) continued to grow, developing into small independent kingdoms with powerful, often rival, Newari (nuh-WAH-ree) rulers. These kings had absolute power; they were believed to be incarnations of the Hindu god Vishnu. Under their rule the caste divisions in society became more rigid. Yet they also showed tolerance toward followers of Buddhism.

In the last years of the fourteenth century, King Jayasthitimalla took control of the three towns. Under his rule the whole Kathmandu Valley was united. The Malla kingdom reached its height under his grandson, Yakshamalla, in the fifteenth century.

The Malla period, especially during the fourteenth and fifteenth centuries, is often seen as a great time in Nepali history. The kingdom was growing more powerful and wealthy. Architects constructed many of Nepal's finest buildings, while skilled craftspeople created exquisite woodcarvings and stone sculptures. Newari language and culture flourished.

The Shah Dynasty

After Yakshamalla, political rivalry divided and weakened the Mallas for nearly two hundred years. The tiny hill kingdom of Gorkhā (GOER-kah) was becoming stronger. Its leaders, who claimed descent from Rajput warriors of India, coveted the wealthy Kathmandu Valley. Gorkhā's greatest and most ruthless leader, King Prithvi Narayan Shah (reigned 1743–1775), besieged and then conquered the valley towns. From Kathmandu, Prithvi and his successors began wars of expansion through much of the Himalayan (hih-mah-LAE-uhn) region.

In 1792 Gorkhā expansion toward Tibet was halted by the Chinese. In the early nineteenth century, expansion to the south, in particular into the fertile Terai (tuh-RIE) region, brought them into conflict with the British, who were becoming powerful in

Kathmandu founded	The Mallas, a Newari dynasty, rule	Nepal at war with British; Nepal defeated and forced to give up territory; boundaries of modern-day Nepal set	Long period of isolation begins	Kot Massacre; Jung Bahadur Rana seizes power
900s	**1200s–1700s**	**1814–1816**	**early 1800s**	**1846**

the Indian subcontinent. After a disastrous two-year war against the British, Nepal was forced to give up territory in the east and west, and most of the Terai. The boundaries of modern-day Nepal became set. The country then followed a policy of complete isolation from the outside world for more than 130 years.

The Ranas

Palace intrigues and power struggles culminated in the Kot Massacre of 1846, in which many of the most powerful men in the kingdom were murdered. An army general, Jung Bahadur Rana, who may have instigated the massacre, seized power. He took complete control of Nepal, establishing a hereditary line of "prime ministers" who ruled Nepal for the next hundred years. The royal family was stripped of all authority.

The Ranas introduced some reforms into the kingdom. Slavery and forced labor were abolished, and the legal system was revised, but the majority of Nepalis continued to live in extreme poverty, had few rights, and had no access to education or medical facilities. Members of the Ranas' court lived in great luxury and extravagance. Economic development was held back, opposition was suppressed, and most Nepalis remained isolated and unaware of changes taking place in the outside world.

The palace of Gorkhā in the ancient capital of the Gorkhā kingdom, from where King Prithvi Narayan Shah set out to conquer and unify all of Nepal.

The Second Half of the Twentieth Century

Major changes in bordering countries had profound and long-lasting effects on Nepal. The new communist government of China (see CHINA) annexed Tibet in 1950, leading to an influx of Tibetan refugees into Nepal. Nepal's powerful neighbor, India, became independent in 1947, and the support that the British had given the Ranas was gone. Indian democracy inspired demands for democracy in Nepal, and the Nepali Congress Party was established. It forced the Ranas to share power, while King Tribhuvan took power

China annexes Tibet, leading to influx of Tibetan refugees into Nepal	Riots in Kathmandu; King Birendra introduces some democracy	Maoist guerrillas begin waging a "people's war"
1950	**1979**	**1990s**

as a constitutional monarch. In 1959 parliamentary elections resulted in a majority for the Congress Party.

In 1960 Tribhuvan's son and successor, King Mahendra, decided that the experiment in democracy was not working. He suspended parliament, banned political parties, and reestablished unlimited royal power. He also introduced a system of basic democracy, based on village councils, or *panchayats* (PAHN-chie-uhtz).

Simmering discontent over poverty, government corruption, and the slow rate of development finally erupted in 1979 with riots in Kathmandu. King Birendra, the son and successor of King Mahendra, introduced some reforms and moves toward democracy. In reality, though, the king retained much of his power. By 1990 continuing strikes and street protests forced Birendra to agree to a new constitution, reinstate political parties, and accept the role of constitutional monarch. The 1990s saw a series of elected governments, including coalitions of different political parties. Meanwhile, Maoist guerrillas began waging a people's war in the hills of Nepal, with the aim of overthrowing the Hindu monarchy.

The New Millennium

At the beginning of the twenty-first century, democracy in Nepal seemed increasingly fragile. In 2001 most of the royal family, including King Birendra, were murdered by the king's oldest son, Dipendra. Birendra's brother, Gyanendra, succeeded to the throne. The new king declared a state of emergency in 2002 and dismissed the elected prime minister. The increasing disaffection of the Nepali people and the growing power of the Maoist rebels left the country on the verge of civil war. Hopes for peace rose at the beginning of 2003, when a cease-fire was agreed between the government and the Maoists.

The Royal Murders

On June 1, 2001, Crown Prince Dipendra, heir to the throne of Nepal, took an automatic rifle and massacred his father, mother, and seven other members of the royal family. He then turned the gun on himself. In the hospital, Dipendra was declared king, following royal protocol, but died three days later.

Fueled by alcohol and drugs, Dipendra's terrible actions seem to have been triggered by a quarrel with his parents over the woman he hoped to marry. The Nepali people were deeply shocked. Many believed the king to be a living god. At first the authorities tried to cover up the truth, and many Nepalis suspected a conspiracy. Thousands took to the streets in mourning and in protest against the government.

Peoples and Languages

The mix of peoples in Nepal is complex and often confusing. There are more than thirty-five ethnic groups, all with their own distinctive customs and dialects. The

King Birendra is murdered by his eldest son; Gyanendra succeeds to the throne	King Gyanendra declares state of emergency	A cease-fire is agreed between the government and the Maoist rebels
2001	**2002**	**2003**

majority of Nepalis originally came from India or from the Tibetan region, yet there is often confusion about where different peoples actually originated. Nepalis can be divided into three main groups: Tibeto-Nepalese, Indo-Nepalese, and indigenous Nepalese.

People who live in the High Himalayas are mostly Tibeto-Nepalese and include the Thakali (tah-KAH-lee) and Sherpa (SHOOR-pah) peoples. Most practice Buddhism and have a culture similar to that of Tibet. In central Nepal, where the land is more fertile and more people have settled, there has been a greater mixing of customs, languages, and religious beliefs. Tibeto-Nepalese who live here include the Tamang, Rai, Limbu, Gurung, and Magar peoples. Their religious practices often mix Buddhism and Hinduism.

The Newar people of the Kathmandu Valley in central Nepal may also be classified as Tibeto-Nepalese in origin, although over the centuries they have blended both Tibetan and Indian cultural influences and made them uniquely their own. Some Newari are Buddhists, but most practice Hinduism and its caste system with Buddhist influences. Newari also have their own distinct language. The influence of Newari in Nepali history and culture is far greater than their population size of more than one million would indicate.

Indo-Nepalese in central Nepal include the Bahuns (buh-HOONZ) and the Chhetris (SHEHT-rees), who today make up about one-third of the population of Nepal. They

A young girl gives the traditional Nepali greeting, clasping both hands together and saying "Namaste," which means both "hello" and "goodbye."

are descended from high-caste Hindu families who fled India several hundred years ago after the Muslim invasions.

In the Terai region of southern Nepal, there are smaller communities who are believed to be the descendants of the earliest indigenous peoples. The largest group is the Tharu (TAH-roo). They practice traditional religion, but are influenced by Hinduism. There are also other, smaller, Indo-Nepalese groups, including small Muslim communities. In recent times, as the Terai has been developed for agriculture and some industry, a greater mix of peoples has begun to move into the region.

The official language is Nepali, which is spoken by most people. There are more than a dozen other languages and many different dialects. About two-thirds of the

The Gurkhas

The legendary Gurkha (GOOR-kah) soldiers of Nepal have fought bravely for the British army since the nineteenth century. The selection process for the British Brigade of Gurkhas is one of the toughest in the world.

The Gurkhas are not a separate ethnic group but are drawn mainly from Tibeto-Nepalese peoples, such as the Magar, Gurung, Limbu, and Rai. The name Gurkha *comes from the kingdom of Gorkhā, which was famed for its brave and loyal warriors.*

The Gurkhas' motto is "Better to die than be a coward." Although today they fight with the most modern weapons, they always carry the traditional Gurkha curved knife, the kukri *(KOO-kree). Tradition has it that the kukri drawn in battle had always to draw blood, either of the enemy or of the Gurkha warrior himself.*

Gurkha soldiers during World War I, in which over 200,000 Gurkhas fought alongside British troops. Here they display their traditional curved knife, the kukri.

Economy and Resources

Nepal is a poor country. It is estimated to be the twelfth poorest country in the world, and the poorest in south Asia. In recent years the government has sought to modernize the economy, for example, through improving farming methods and investing in education, transportation, and communications. However, several factors, above all population growth and political instability, have held back economic development. The mountainous nature of much of Nepal also makes it difficult to develop a modern transportation system.

Nepal's economy is largely based on agriculture. More than eight out of ten Nepalis depend on small-scale farming for their livelihood. The main food crops that farmers grow include rice, beans, corn, grains such as wheat and barley, potatoes, and oilseeds. The main agricultural areas

population describe Nepali as their first language. Related to Hindi, the written form, known as Devanagari (deh-vah-nuh-GAH-ree), is based on Sanskrit (SAN-skriht). Most literature in Nepal is written in Nepali, but there is also a strong literary tradition in Newari. The Newari language has its own alphabet. English is also spoken by many people who work in government and business, especially in important tourist centers such as Kathmandu and Pokharā (poe-KAH-ruh).

are the Kathmandu Valley and increasingly the Terai region. Yet only about one-fifth of the land in Nepal can be farmed, and that land is under severe strain from a growing population. Many families also keep livestock, such as sheep, goats, and poultry. Cows provide milk and dung, which is used as fertilizer, while oxen may be used for plowing. In the Himalayas the main domestic animal is the yak.

Most of Nepal's energy comes from fuel wood, which has led to serious deforestation. The country's fast-flowing rivers offer huge potential for the future development of hydroelectric power, but Nepal is not highly industrialized. Many goods are produced by small-scale industries. Larger industries are mostly located in the Kathmandu Valley and the Terai and concentrate on food processing, cement, woolen carpets, and textiles. The tourist industry is extremely important to Nepal's economy.

Terrace farming in the hills of Nepal. Here a farmer uses oxen to pull a simple wooden plow—just as his forefathers did—before planting his rice crop.

Education and Health

Current estimates indicate that only around 30 percent of Nepalis can read and write. The literacy rate is higher in urban areas and also among men. Until fifty years ago only one out of every hundred children attended school.

In recent years the government has invested in a major expansion of education. Elementary education is now free and, in theory, compulsory. Children start school at age six and may go on to high school at eleven. However, there are not enough qualified teachers, classrooms are overcrowded, and few schools have sufficient textbooks. In rural areas there is a high dropout rate because families often need children to work on the land or help out at home. In the towns there are also fee-paying schools, for those parents who can afford it, but the standard of these schools varies, and some appear to be run more for profit than for education.

Life expectancy for most Nepalis has increased in recent years, but at fifty-nine

A young Nepali girl carries a heavy load of wood for fuel. Nepal's mountainous terrain and lack of roads mean that many goods have to be carried on people's backs.

Daily Life

For most Nepalis, irrespective of which ethnic group they belong to, the patterns of daily life center on the land, the family home, the village community, and religion.

A majority of Nepalis are small-scale farmers. Today many families only have tiny plots to farm, a result of the rapidly growing population and the traditional system of dividing up land. They often have to walk long distances to reach their land or to collect water. Farming is hard work, with little modern equipment and heavy reliance on human labor. In addition, many poor Nepalis do not own their farms but work land belonging to wealthy landowners. Families are often forced to borrow money just to survive, and personal debt has become a serious problem.

years for men and women it remains low. In rural areas less than one in five Nepalis has access to clean water and sanitation. Many Nepalis also have deprived diets and are, therefore, prone to infection and disease, including tuberculosis, goiter, and leprosy.

In the last years of the twentieth century, the government made major efforts to expand health services, including the provision of hospitals, health centers, and village-based health workers, but the mountainous nature of much of Nepal means that rural families often have to walk for several hours to reach their nearest health center.

Ayurveda (ie-yuhr-VAE-duh), an ancient system of Hindu medicine, is used by many Nepalis to stay healthy and to treat sickness. Ayurvedic practitioners advise on diet and lifestyle and prescribe medicines made from herbs, plants, and minerals.

Nepalis may also turn to medicine men, the practitioners of traditional folk medicine.

Different Peoples, Different Traditions

Daily life among the peoples of the High Himalayas, such as the Thakalis and Sherpas, is shaped both by the mountainous landscape in which they live and their Tibetan inheritance. Life there is tough, with a harsh climate. Many families grow potatoes or grain crops on the poor soil and keep herds of yak and sheep. Many lead a seminomadic lifestyle, moving to high-mountain grazing with their flocks during the summer months. During the winter months some Himalayan peoples migrate to the towns of the Kathmandu Valley and the Terai to find seasonal work. Different groups of hill peoples also work as porters, innkeepers, guides, or traders. In hill communities women usually have more freedom than Indo-Nepaleses or Newari women. In a few groups in the far north, polyandry — where women take more than one husband — is still practiced.

Among the Bahuns and Chhetris, the practices and social structures of Hinduism, particularly the caste system, shape much of daily life. Both groups are high-caste Hindus: the Bahuns are the priest caste, and the Chhetris are the warrior caste. In the Kathmandu Valley the Bahuns often work in government or business. Many Chhetris also serve in government or in the army. Nepal's royal family is Chhetris. Outside the valley, both Bahuns and Chhetris are often just small-scale farmers, living in scattered settlements.

The Newari of the Kathmandu Valley are essentially urban dwellers. They often work in business or in different trades, but many also go out into the fields of the valley every day to farm. Newari families

In old Kathmandu, Durbar Square and the surrounding streets are packed with houses and temples. The square has more than fifty temples and monuments.

Newari Guthis

Guthis (GOO-tees) are social and religious organizations that, in different ways, provide community support to individuals and families within Newari society. They reflect the importance of community life to the Newari, and most adults belong to several guthis. Guthi meetings may be simply social get-togethers, but Guthis also organize committees to plan local festivals, look after the sick and elderly in the community, arrange funerals, and raise funds for facilities in the neighborhood. Guthis play a vital role in protecting the cultural traditions and important social values of the Newari people.

live in closely packed brick houses, three or four stories high and often built around a small courtyard. Religious shrines and temples mingle with family homes. Individuals within Newari society are born

into one of more than sixty different occupational castes, including priests, tailors, farmers, stonemasons, and sweepers. Newari live in large families, often with three generations living in one house. With so many people all living under one roof, the patterns of daily family life, full of particular obligations and duties, are clear.

Tradition and Change

Nepal has no large cities. The largest town, the capital Kathmandu, is estimated to have a population of around half a million. There are a number of new towns developing in the Terai region.

Traditional ways—the extended family, religion, the village, or neighborhood community—still have a strong hold for most Nepalis, but many, especially the young, have begun to question aspects of the way Nepali society works. The poor are growing poorer. They see those who have held traditional power mismanaging the economy, while doing nothing to rectify the ever-widening divide in society.

The Daily Diet

Dhal bhat tarkari (dahl-baht-tah-KAH-ree)—boiled rice, lentil sauce, and vegetables cooked with spices—is often regarded as the national dish of Nepal. Rice is a favorite in the Nepali diet, but many families, especially in the mountains, can only afford *dhedo* (DAE-doe), a staple based on flour mixed with water. Few people eat meat on a daily basis. Meat dishes are consumed on special occasions, such as festivals or weddings. Most Nepali Hindus avoid beef, but are not strictly vegetarian, while Buddhists will eat meat, but they cannot kill animals. That must be done by a non-Buddhist.

Many Nepali dishes are variations of Indian cooking, but there are also regional dishes. In the mountains, Tibetan-influenced foods include *thupka* (THOOP-kah), a thick soup, and *momo* (MOE-moe), steamed or fried meat wrapped in dough.

Buffalo, cow, or yak milk is used to make yogurt and butter, known as *ghee* (GEE), for cooking. The near rancid butter is used to flavor salt tea. Other beverages include sweet, milky tea and salt or sweet *lassi* (LAH-see), made with yogurt. *Chang* (CHANG) is home-brewed beer made from barley, while *raksi* (RAHK-see) is a strong, grain-based liquor.

A woman prepares a meal in a restaurant kitchen. Most Nepali food, always freshly made, is cooked in simple kitchens with the most basic equipment.

A Hindu holy man, or sadhu. Sadhus give up their homes, family life, and worldly possessions to live a simple life of fasting and prayer.

Religion and Culture

Nepal is the only country in the world that calls itself a Hindu kingdom. Estimates suggest that nearly 90 percent of the population is Hindu, while many of the remaining 10 percent are Tibetan Buddhists. There are also small numbers of Muslims, Christians, and followers of traditional religions.

In practice, there is much mixing of Hindu and Buddhist beliefs. Followers of both faiths often worship at each other's temples. Nepali Hindus regard the Buddha as an incarnation of the Hindu god Vishnu. Nepali Buddhists think of the Hindu trinity of gods (Brahma, Vishnu, and Shiva) as different aspects of the Buddha. The caste system influences many aspects of daily life, both for Hindus and non-Hindus.

The Kumari on her throne. Although she is regarded as a goddess, life can be difficult for a Kumari girl—it is said to be unlucky to marry a former Kumari.

Kumari Devi – The Living Goddess

Nepalis believe that the Kumari Devi (koo-MAH-ree DAE-vee), a young girl chosen at the age of about five, is an incarnation of a Hindu goddess. In order to become the living goddess, young girls must go through a series of tests, and attributes such as the color of her eyes, the shape of her teeth, and the sound of her voice are also fundamental. The true Kumari must be perfect in every way. She must also endure a terrifying ordeal, in a darkened room with masked demons and slaughtered buffalo heads, and show no fear.

Once chosen, the Kumari lives in the house of the living goddess in Kathmandu and only leaves it for particular festivals. Her feet must never touch the ground, so she is carried everywhere in a chariot. When the Kumari reaches puberty, she is no longer a goddess, and a new Kumari is chosen.

Losar Festival in Kathmandu celebrates the Buddhist New Year. Crowds gather around monks in vermilion and saffron robes, who are making offerings before a holy image.

Families may ask a Buddhist monk to officiate at some religious ceremonies and a Brahmin (Hindu) priest at others.

Festivals

Nepal has a wealth of festivals throughout the year. Most are Hindu or Buddhist celebrations, although followers of one religion often take part in the other's festivals. Some are large, nationwide festivals—others are more local. Most Nepali festivals follow the lunar calendar, so they fall on different days each year.

The biggest of all the Hindu festivals is *Dussehra* (doo-SAE-rah), which takes place during the end of September and early October, after the monsoon. It celebrates the triumph of good over evil, in particular the fearless Hindu goddess Durga, who defeated the buffalo demon. Dussehra lasts for at least ten days, ending on the full

moon. Much of Dussehra is spent quietly at home with family, but there are also different events on each day of the festival—Brahmin priests plant barley seeds, and there are kite-flying competitions and military parades. On the ninth day thousands of animals are sacrificed to Durga. Other major Hindu festivals include *Tihar* (tih-HAHR), also known as *Diwali* (dih-WAH-lee), the festival of lights, and *Holi* (HOE-lee), the festival of colors.

An important festival for Nepali Buddhists is *Losar* (loe-SAHR), the New Year festival. Losar begins with the rising of the new moon in February. Families dress in their best clothes and celebrate with feasting, family visits, and the sharing of gifts. Streets and homes are decorated with brightly colored prayer flags.

Teej – The Festival of Women

This unique festival is celebrated throughout the Kathmandu Valley, but above all at Pashupatinath (pah-shoo-PAH-tee-nahth), a temple dedicated to the god Shiva and the most important Hindu temple in Nepal. Women come to seek blessing from Shiva and his consort, the goddess Parvati. Married women honor their husbands and wear the red and gold saris in which they were married. They ask Parvati and Shiva to bless them with a long and devoted married life. Unmarried women ask the gods to bring them a good husband.

This is a joyous festival that opens with feasting, dancing, and folk songs. On the second and sometimes the third day, the women fast. They also take ritual cleansing dips in the river.

recently died. Masked dancers reenact Indra's victory over various demons. The people of Kathmandu, including the king, also pay homage to the Kumari Devi, the living goddess.

Music and Dance

Most music and dance in Nepal is religious in nature, and both are essential elements of Nepali festivals. Nepal has a rich and varied musical tradition, a reflection of its ethnic diversity. Strongly influenced by Indian classical music, Nepali musicians often play instruments of Indian origin, including the *sarangi* (suh-RAHN-jee: like a viola), the tabla (TAH-blah: a pair of drums), flutes, and cymbals.

Traveling folk musicians and dancers entertain village children, playing traditional instruments—long horns, both straight and curved, and large drums.

Celebrations often center around monasteries, where Buddhist monks offer prayers and act out special dances. The great stupas (STOO-pahs)—stone structures built to remember the Buddha's life and teachings—of Boudhanath (BOO-dah-nahth) and Swayambhunath (SWIE-uhm-boo-nahth), in Kathmandu, provide a special focus for Losar celebrations.

A festival celebrated by both Hindus and Buddhists is *Indra Jatra* (IHN-drah ZHAH-truh), held in late August or early September in the Kathmandu Valley. It honors Indra, the god of rain, and also those who have

The all-seeing eyes of the Buddha above the stupa of Swayambhunath in Kathmandu. The white mound of the stupa represents the four elements—earth, fire, air, and water.

Professional folk musicians, known as *gaines* (GAE-nuhz), once went from village to village, singing religious songs and telling stories. Whole families traveled together, and their music traditions were handed down through the generations. Today the gaines are beginning to die out. Modern professional musicians, the *damais* (duh-MIE-uhz), however, are very popular, especially at weddings. The damais all belong to the Newari. They often wear special uniforms and play in large, loud bands.

Sacred Tibetan music, often heard at Buddhist festivals and religious sites, features chanting, which may be accompanied by long horns, trumpets, flutes, and conches (large shells). Nepal also has a long tradition of both classical and folk dance. Classical dancing is associated above all with the Newari. Folk dances and dramas may have important

religious elements and are often linked to the rhythms of rural life—the seasons, the harvest, and romance.

Dancers perform in villages, outside temples, and in street processions during festivals. The different dances often tell stories of the gods, evil spirits, and demons, and the eventual victory of good over evil. They are dramatic and colorful, with costumes and masks. The masked dances of Bhaktapur in the Kathmandu Valley are particularly famous.

Art and Architecture

Religion has inspired many of Nepal's finest architectural and artistic achievements. The most distinctive and impressive Nepali architecture belongs to the Newar people. They developed their own unique style, a skillful blend of both Hindu and Buddhist influences. The Newari architecture of the valley towns—above all Kathmandu, Lalitpur, and Bhaktapur—is still mostly medieval, with hundreds of temples and palaces. The style of these buildings dates from the later Malla period, although many have been reconstructed following earthquake damage. The most beautiful are the pagoda-style temples. Each pagoda temple has a sequence of roofs, which get smaller as they go up. The style of *shikara* (shih-KAH-ruh) temples is different, showing a strong Indian influence.

The famous stupas of Boudhanath and Swayambhunath in Kathmandu were built some two thousand years ago and are Nepal's most important Buddhist architectural monuments. Stupas are large religious shrines in mound form, and may contain relics. Above the Swayambhunath and Boudhanath stupas are towers, and on each side of the tower are huge painted eyes. These represent the all-seeing eyes of the Buddha, watching over the universe.

Traditionally, much Nepali art has been linked to the decoration of temples and palaces. It is expressed in stone sculptures, in wooden carvings around temple doors and windows, in metalwork, and in paintings. In the Kathmandu Valley the most skilled artists have come from the Newari. There are different occupational castes for different arts, such as stonemasons, painters, and metalworkers. Buddhist artists paint or embroider *thangkas*, scroll banners that hang in temples, monasteries, and family shrines. Their vivid colors depict images of the Buddha or scenes from his life.

These traditional arts are becoming rare today. More items are produced for the tourist trade, and the quality has declined. However, some of the skills remain and are called upon for restoration work on Nepal's ancient temples.

Practical arts, above all the decoration of everyday household items, have long been part of Nepali culture. Mass-produced goods have replaced many of these hand-decorated items. A local art still popular today is seen in the colorful paintings adorning many bicycle rickshaws, buses, and trucks.

A brightly decorated bicycle rickshaw. In Kathmandu rickshaws are the local taxi cab. Their drivers are skilled at negotiating the crowded, narrow streets.

Glossary

animism the belief that things in nature, such as trees, mountains, and the sky, have souls or consciousness.

archaeology the scientific study of ancient cultures through the examination of their material remains, such as fossil relics, monuments, and tools.

Brahmin the highest Hindu caste, the members of which are priests and scholars.

caste system the Hindu system of organizing society into classes.

censorship the banning of all or part of materials, such as plays, movies, or publications, considered unsuitable for their audience.

communist a believer in communism, a theory that suggests that all property belongs to the community and that work should be organized for the common good.

constitution a written statement outlining the laws of a country, stating people's rights and duties and establishing the powers and duties of the government.

constitutional monarch a political system where the head of state is a king or queen, ruling to the extent allowed by a constitution.

deforestation the clearing of forests.

democracy a state ruled by the people; a state in which government is carried out by representatives elected by the public.

famine a severe shortage of food, usually resulting in widespread hunger.

fermentation the process in which a microorganism breaks down a substance into simpler ones, especially alcohol from yeast and sugar.

fossil fuel a fuel such as coal, oil, or natural gas that is formed in the earth from plant or animal remains.

goiter an enlargement of the thyroid gland creating a swelling of the neck.

guerrilla a member of an irregular fighting force whose tactics include ambushes, surprise attacks, and sabotage rather than intense, close battles with the enemy.

house arrest a legal confinement in which people who have been arrested are not allowed to leave their homes.

hunter-gatherer somebody who lives by no other means than hunting and gathering.

hydroelectric of or relating to production of electricity from waterpower. The force of a waterfall or dammed river may be used to produce electricity in a power station.

indigenous originating in and typical of a region or country.

lacquer a coating, such as a varnish, that dries quickly into a shiny layer.

landlocked closed in completely by land.

leprosy an infectious disease that attacks the skin and nerves and can cause deformities and loss of sensation, weight, and strength.

Mahabharata an Indian epic poem dating back more than two thousand years.

Maoism the theory and practice of Mao Tse-tung's policies.

molybdenum a hard, silver-colored metallic element used to strengthen and harden steel.

monastery a place where a community of monks or nuns live and work.

Nobel Peace Prize an international prize awarded annually for outstanding achievement in promoting world peace. Established by the will of Alfred Nobel (1833–1869), a Swedish chemist, engineer, and industrialist.

nomadic describes people who do not have a permanent home but instead move from place to place, usually in search of pasture for their animals.

pagoda a richly decorated temple.

propaganda the spreading of ideas and information by a government or organization with the purpose of furthering or damaging a cause.

rebel somebody who fights against their own government in order to change the political system.

sari a garment, worn especially by women from the Indian subcontinent, consisting of a long piece of material folded around the body.

slash-and-burn a form of agriculture where trees and vegetation are cut down and burned in order to plant crops in their place.

steppes land covered in grass in a region of extreme temperature range.

stupa a Buddhist shrine, usually in the shape of a dome, that houses a relic or marks the location of an auspicious event.

tuberculosis an infectious disease caused by a bacterium and usually marked by weight loss, fever, coughing, and difficulty in breathing.

tungsten a gray, hard metallic element with a very high melting point that is used especially for electrical purposes and to harden other metals and blends of metals, such as steel.

United Nations an alliance, founded in 1945, which today includes most of the countries in the world. Its aim is to encourage international cooperation and peace.

warlord a powerful military leader operating outside the control of government.

World Bank a specialized agency of the United Nations that guarantees loans to member nations for the purpose of reconstruction and development.

World War I a conflict that broke out in Europe in 1914. The Entente powers, or Allies, (which included the United Kingdom, France, and Russia) fought the Central Powers (which included Austria-Hungary, Germany, and Turkey). The United States joined the Allies in 1917. The war ended in 1918.

World War II a war that began in Europe in 1939 and spread to involve many other countries worldwide. It ended in 1945. The United Kingdom, France, the Soviet Union, the United States, Canada, Australia, New Zealand, and other European countries fought against Germany, Italy, and Japan.

Further Reading

Internet Sites

Look under Countries A to Z in the Atlapedia Online Web Site at
> http://www.atlapedia.com

Use the drop-down menu to select a country on the CIA World Factbook Web Site at
> http://www.odci.gov/cia/publications/factbook

Browse the Table of Contents in the Library of Congress Country Studies Web Site at
> http://lcweb2.loc.gov/frd/cs/cshome.html

Use the Country Locator Maps in the World Atlas Web Site at
> http://www.worldatlas.com/aatlas/world.htm

Look under the alphabetical country listing using the Infoplease Atlas at
> http://www.infoplease.com/countries.html

Use the drop-down menu to select a country using E-Conflict™ World Encyclopedia at
> http://www.emulateme.com

Look under the alphabetical country listing in the Yahooligans Around the World Directory at
> http://www.yahooligans.com/Around_the_World/Countries

Choose the part of the world you're interested in, then scroll down to choose the country using the Geographia Web Site at
> http://www.geographia.com

Mongolia

Hanson, Jennifer. *Mongolia (Nations in Transition)*. New York: Facts on File, 2003.

Pang, Guek-Cheng. *Mongolia (Cultures of the World)*. Tarrytown, NY: Benchmark Books, 1999.

Myanmar

Fisher, Frederick, and Pauline Khng. *Myanmar (Countries of the World)*. Milwaukee, WI: Gareth Stevens, 2000.

Yip, Dora, and Pauline Khng. *Welcome to Myanmar (Welcome to My Country)*. Milwaukee, WI: Gareth Stevens, 2001.

Nepal

Burbank, Jon. *Nepal (Cultures of the World)*. Tarrytown, NY: Benchmark Books, 2002.

Index

Page numbers in *italic* indicate illustrations.

Page numbers in *italic* indicate illustrations.